While
Someone Else
Is Eating

While Someone Else Is Eating

Edited and with an Introduction by
Earl Shorris

Eric Etheridge and Sylvia Sasson
Associate Editors

ANCHOR PRESS / DOUBLEDAY
Garden City, New York
1984

AAV 1840

"Segundo's Benefits," "One of the Lucky Ones," "The Empty House," "Roosters and Saints," "It's Very Hard to Say I'm Poor," and "Christmas Eve" first appeared in *The Nation*.

Copyright © 1983, 1984 by the Nation Associates, Inc.

Library of Congress Cataloging in Publication Data
Main entry under title:

While someone else is eating.

1. Poor—United States—Collected works.   2. United States—Economic policy—1981- —Collected works. I. Shorris, Earl, 1936- . II. Etheridge,Eric. III. Sasson, Sylvia.
HC110.P6W49   1984   330.973'0927   82–45606
ISBN 0-385-18418-2

FOREWORD

ALL MAGAZINE EDITORS ARE CURSED WITH FRIENDS WHO have good ideas. If they are true friends, the ideas will be vague, expensive, ambitious, and impractical, but with just enough merit to ensnare the editor. Victor Navasky, the editor of *The Nation*, is cursed with more friends than most editors, since he is that extraordinary creature in the world, a man without a dark side.

In approaching Victor with the idea that eventually became this book, I followed the rules of friendship, beginning the conversation with a complaint about the magazine. Good editors take careful note of such complaints; great editors sleep.

Victor emerged well rested to listen to a suggestion for a series of articles to be written by novelists and poets, rather than journalists. The idea was to ask writers of accomplishment to work at *Nation* rates. Victor knew that would not work; moreover, he pointed out that it would be unfair, for the writers would be putting in weeks of work on the articles. He suggested that we find a publisher who would be interested in making a book of the series. An advance against royalties could be used to pay the writers.

At last I was able to offer a practical suggestion: Loretta Barrett. There was no doubt that she would understand the idea immediately and that she would be sympathetic to it. While Loretta is not an ideologue by any means, she is a woman for whom both compassion and new ideas are serious parts of life. Our presentation to her was never completed. Before we arrived at the arguments for the book, she was talking about titles, scheduling, shaping the book through geographic distribution, and how the very unevenness of the collection would make it more readable and more affecting.

Elizabeth Pochoda, who was then literary editor of *The Nation*, was to have been coeditor of the book. It was she who suggested the names of many of the writers whose work appears in these pages. Unfortunately, she left *The Nation* and the project early on, to become an editor of another magazine—for which this book no doubt suffers.

It is not easy to put together a book such as this, for poets and novelists are not used to working to deadlines or to dealing with the world as it is, rather than as it can be invented. Eric Etheridge, of *The Nation*, and Sylvia Sasson have done most of the real work of putting the series and this book together. They are orderly, careful, appreciating people. I have relied on their judgment, their talent, and their patience. Sylvia kept the project alive when I was unable to work on it for several months. Eric shaped the pieces for publication in the magazine. Both contributed to the light editing that was done.

All of us are grateful to Paul Aron, of Doubleday, for guiding the work through the publishing process.

Many writers and several literary agents were helpful in putting this book together, among them Rodolfo Anaya, Anne Bernays, Carol Bly, Josephine Carson, Laurie Colwin, Bette Howland, Reynolds Price, Lois Wallace, and Sol Yurick. I wish that everything they suggested or began or considered had worked out.

E.S.

Contents

About suffering they were never wrong,
The Old Masters: how well they understood
Its human position; how it takes place
While someone else is eating or opening a
window or just walking dully along

W . H . AUDEN

While
Someone Else
Is Eating

EDITOR'S INTRODUCTION

JOHN STEINBECK, RICHARD WRIGHT, JACK CONROY, JAMES Agee, Nelson Algren, Eudora Welty, and all the others, including the photographers and the editors and the ones who got lost, surely were sufficient. Poverty has been described. Americans cannot help but know what it means to be out of work, to accept charity, to suffer hunger or, worse, to watch one's children suffer hunger, to be sick without care, to be homeless, to be alone, to die alone. After the last Depression, the rich and reasonable people of America surely will no longer permit massive unemployment. They would not abandon the social programs that raise the quality of life for the poorest to some level not unjustly distant from the minimum required to imagine happiness. Surely the American people would not again permit such failures of human society, if they knew, if they understood.

This is an optimistic book, an attempt.

Who is to say what people know or believe of each other's lives? The makers and takers of opinion polls claim to know something, but what poll surveys joy or pain, beatitude or rage? Is there a statistic that delineates exactly what you think of God? Perhaps people do not believe what they see on television, perhaps the dots are too far apart or the duration of the stories is too brief; perhaps it is all understood as a series of comic situations? Perhaps people do not know.

If people knew, this would be a desperate book.

Once, when we were young, or was it earlier on, governments spoke of full employment, and then of 4 percent unemployment as full employment and then of 6 percent unemployment as full employment, and somewhere along the way it turned out that one or two million people weren't counted, because they were discouraged and not looking for work, rather than unemployed. Recently, 8 percent unemployed plus the discouraged has been discussed as full employment, meaning that we would consider ourselves successful as a society if only one person in ten were desperate.

It is a long time since the legions of Rome knew decimation as an awesome punishment for the worst of crimes.

Inside the legion the horror of decimation was inescapable. Apparently, the same quality of impression cannot be accomplished in a society of two hundred and thirty million people spread across a country twenty-five hundred miles wide. Something is lacking in the means for understanding. Perhaps it is proximity. The poor are so far away; an outdoor antenna is required just to get a picture of them.

No one knows how many Americans are poor. One family in ten? How many children? One in seven perhaps, thirty-four million? Those are the numbers published by the Congressional Budget Office. And so many of the poor are children. The poor always seem to have children. Perhaps that's what makes them poor. Recently, the definition of poverty has been challenged. Some say that the person who spends food stamps in the grocery store may not be poor.

In the decimation of a Roman legion no soldier was so far from one who died that he was spared the sensory experience of his comrade's death. The electronic dots may be incapable of producing the same experience, for there was an attempt by the television networks to note the concurrent decimations of poverty and unemployment. Dan Rather, of CBS, has been accused of "soup-kitchen journalism," probably meaning that he regularly shows his viewers pictures of lines of people waiting to accept free meals or parcels of food from private charities. But no public howl follows such glimpses of desperation.

Magazines have not been accused of "soup-kitchen journalism," because those magazines not limited to the services of pleasure tend toward abstraction or analysis. Politically conservative magazines generally write at a higher level of abstraction than either liberal or centrist magazines, and with good reason: it is very difficult to stand amid a host of malnourished children and claim their suffering is the result of man's justice under God. On the Left, there is an assumption of the reader's awareness of existing conditions, as if that made it so.

The task of putting the reality of other people before the

public seems still to fall to the daily newspaper, and even though newspapers have changed, devoting more space to service articles, often limiting their reporters to very short pieces almost in the style of television, some have tried to convey at least a part of the reality of Reaganism. Among these, the New York *Times* has often devoted the most space and effort.

It was out of just such an effort that this book was conceived. A New York *Times* reporter was describing the life of a woman living on welfare. The reporter listed the woman's budget down to the last cent. Every aspect of the woman's daily itinerary was listed. Along the way, the reporter said that in winter the woman shared a pair of boots with her daughter. Nothing more was said of this sharing. It was not considered meaningful, not in the way of food or shelter.

What might have been written if the observer had been Tolstoy instead of the reporter from the New York *Times?* Reporters and artists are gifted alike with senses, but artists are free to give us their gift, even if it is only for the duration of a couplet or at most for the few days of living with a novel.

Many years ago, in Moscow, an editor of the *Literary Gazette* told me that censorship of literary works in the Soviet Union was derived from their awareness of the effect literature could have on the people: Tolstoy and Dostoevski, the editor said, may have been as important as Marx and Lenin in bringing about the Russian Revolution. In America, we are twice spared such dangers: we pay little attention to literature, and what literature we do produce now is often not about the common reality; that work is left to journalists.

To give evidence no longer attracts the novelist or the poet, and the journalist has neither the art nor the freedom to give evidence in a manner that captures the conscience of the reader. No matter how the journalist tries to emulate the artist's ability to enter the member of the audience, to make his work a part of the experienced history of that person, the limitations of his craft will defeat him. Journalism succeeds by the very rules that differentiate it from art. To remove the constraints of striving for objectivity, eliminating imaginative speculations and digressions, avoiding ambiguity, maintaining traditional forms, working at a dispassionate distance, straining the work through levels of editors committed to routine language and responses, and so on would be to destroy the dubitable distinction between journalism and propaganda, or worse, between journalism and art.

The question avoided here, so far, is whether journalism or art is more truthful. It does not seem a promising avenue of exploration, for both the artist and the journalist seek, by definition of the art or craft, to convey the truth. The question here is of the most effective method of telling the truth of a particular situation.

The optimism of this book derives from the belief that neither print nor electronic journalism has been effective in making the truth known. It is an optimism of faith in this nation and in the "each other" of America. One must be simply and straightforwardly a patriot to believe that if Tolstoy had encountered the woman who shared a pair of boots with her daughter in winter, he would have written a story that might have affected the politics of our fellow citizens.

To permit patriotism to endure, one must believe that if Americans truly knew of the plight of their fellow citizens, they would not permit it. The poor suffer a merciless, unjust existence because they are hidden, unknown, uninteresting. Perhaps it is the gray homogeneity of the poor that limits the television networks to showing their plight in segments of seventy or ninety seconds. Perhaps it is the sameness of poverty that leads most newspapers to deal with the problem in analytical fashion, by the numbers. It could have been the dullness of living poor that led Oscar Lewis into his terrible slander of Puerto Ricans and all poor people in *La Vida*.

One must either believe in the unknownness of the poor or lose faith in the character of the nation and the great majority of the inhabitants thereof. If the poor are known, felt, understood, then moral men and women have no choice but in their despair to bring down the government and the culture, to begin again, to call for the Flood.

In the beginning of the second quarter of 1983, just as the economy was supposedly coming up from a deep recession or a depression, the federal government announced that one fourth of all the children in America lived at or near the poverty level.

As the stock market established record highs, it was forecast by many economists that total unemployment, including discouraged persons, would remain at or above 10 percent: decimation.

A madness of disjunction has come over us. Apparently, we are no longer able to notice that our neighbors have nothing to eat. Apparently, forty-five seconds of desperation on the evening television news does not seem real to us, or if it looks real, it does not seem common. Apparently, the numbers are simply numbers, abstractions reported in the daily newspaper, numbers that do not apply to us.

It must be so.

If it is not so, we Americans would have done something about it. We did something in the nineteen thirties. Were we so different then? Perhaps the qualities of disbelief and disjunction were not so prevalent. We have been citizens of a nation led by lawyers, soldiers, technicians, and administrators, but we have never before been led by a man who made his life in make-believe. Mr. Reagan brings the cult of antireality to power; he is living proof that the American way may be a deception, that the poor step out of range of the cameras to snack on caviar and champagne. We must believe that those on welfare are cheating; isn't everything make-believe; isn't hunger a sham; aren't snowflakes made of soap? The truth, according to Hollywood, is anything we want it to be, not as in art, surely not as in art, but as in propaganda, the art we have come to call disinformation.

Then, what can be done?

If Tolstoy had met the woman who shared a pair of boots with her daughter in winter . . . If Tolstoy had met her, what would have happened? We do not know; we can only experiment, wondering all the while how it is that Agee and Wright and Steinbeck and Conroy and Algren and Welty and all the rest did not succeed once and for all in putting an end to disinformation by connecting us to the truth of how many people live.

Those writers—artists—succeeded in making reality understood because they did not write about poverty as poverty, they wrote about people and situations greater than economics, about unquantifiable humanity, about themselves and what they knew and how they saw. They ordered the world so that we could and can still understand it; they included us, and they did it so thoroughly that most of us who have read their works are unable to escape what they saw and were and thought and said. They did not only bring the truth to us; because they were artists, they brought us to the truth.

Can artists do so now?

Poverty is not the same as in the Depression of the nineteen thirties. We have progressed: we are a richer nation; we are the most expert of all nations at hiding our poor. We have learned to dress our poor more carefully, to let desperation come more slowly. How poor is a person with a television set? Should a person sell an ancient automobile to qualify for welfare? Should the same standards be applied to illegal immigrants? Why are so many blacks and Hispanics still poor; why aren't they working their way into the middle class? What would Richard Wright or James Agee have thought of some of the people in this book?

How much should government do? What are the minimums of a decent life? If you pity a person, does that make the person poorer?

After the thirties, we are so sophisticated about poverty it has become difficult, nearly impossible to write about people who are poor, to do the artist's work of bringing people to the truth. We are very nearly closed down, made mute by self-consciousness, by fear of the news media, awe at the movies, astonishment at life.

There is a reason for the artist to work again at bringing people to the truth: the old work won't do. It is a new time, with new troubles. Structural unemployment growing out of the automation of factories and offices is, according to *Fortune* magazine, diminishing the middle class. Union busting, which was given new life by Mr. Reagan's dealings with the air traffic controllers, and the unbridled acquisition of smaller companies by conglomerates are also having some effect. The end of America's worldwide economic domination has begun to slow the expansion that provides nourishment to the capitalist system. These are among the causes of the new and unexpected forms of poverty. Mary Lee Settle and John van der Zee found farms so different from what we are accustomed to that we may have difficulty recognizing what we see.

It may not be possible for poets and novelists to speak so openly, so straightforwardly now as in the thirties, for the problems are more complex in the era of many Armageddons. But artists can try. And if this effort fails utterly, if no person on earth is affected by it, none of the writers will have been diminished as artists or citizens or persons.

II

Why do artists tend to be on the Left, by which I mean on the side of both freedom and social justice? Perhaps the muse is moral, or as Sol Yurick corrected me, perhaps the muse is sometimes moral. It is possible. Consideration of the alternative supports the notion. William Buckley, for example, could no more be an artist than an artist could be William Buckley.

In the course of putting together a book like this, in which diversity was one of the criteria by which the writers were chosen, one gains some sense of the nature of writers. I found, with few exceptions, that the hubris of writing itself is sufficient for most artists, which leaves them free to wish life for others, as good citizens must. It pleases me now, as never before, to be part of the category of poets and novelists.

Imagine getting a telephone call from a stranger who asks you to do weeks of work for very little money, with no guarantee of publication either in a magazine of relatively small circulation or in this book. The stranger doesn't work at the magazine or at the publishing house. You don't know his politics except that he opposes the cruelties of Reaganism. What would you do? Most writers said yes.

Since the assignment was purposely vague, to give the series and the book the sense of a community of individuals, each with his or her own style and sensibility, the writers did not know exactly what they had agreed to. The rules were simple: write about real people. Change their names if you like. Please write less than ten thousand words and more than a haiku. For most it would be an exploration of both the self and the world, an essay in the old sense of the word, when it was tentative and could be accused of wildness.

Not every writer said yes, and some of those who did either had a change of heart or are still working on the piece. One of those who said no was Eudora Welty. "Oh, I did that during the last Depression," she said, and went on to say that such a book would be interesting for her students to read, because they sometimes thought her stories were true, which they are, but not in the same way that nonfiction is true.

Most of the writers whose work appears in this book had other things to do: novels, film scripts, teaching, "poebiz." None of them gave much attention to the deal (payments, kill fee, book publication, etc.). I suspect that when the money arrived in the mail they were surprised by the arrival of the check and dismayed by the amount. (Many of them shared the money with the people they wrote about.) Although there were no discussions of the role of artists in society, there was a feeling about most conversations that we were trying to make poets public again, to begin an Athens of rebels in the time of Ronald Reagan's presidency.

I believe that all the writers who participated in the project did so because of their sense of what ought to be and what ought to be said. If artists were on the Right instead of the Left, wouldn't they have concentrated on the deal, abandoning what ought to be to the care of some invisible hand? The overcoming of fate has fascinated the artist since the beginning. Only the rich and powerful are grateful to fate; the poor do not feel befriended by it. In that profound way, artists are the kith of the poor.

III

Since liars have nothing to gain by lying about their lies, one can trust fiction. Similarly, we do not often dream of dreaming or imagine we are imagining, so art can be trusted no matter how one thinks it comes about. The highest achievement of art, it might be argued, is truth, while the highest achievement of journalism can never be more than verisimilitude, by which I mean that the ideal of journalism is to reproduce in language the thing or situation, to be like the object, no more and no less.

But what happens when artists are asked to make something other than truth? Can liars be verisimilitudinous?

Who will be fact checker for Mary Lee Settle? She has made inventions that span decades, centuries! Ron Arias may be trusted to remember South America, where he was a journalist, but what about Texas, where he was born? Who will vouch for the truthfulness of people who have declared themselves liars?

The editor.

The editor will dip into the Faulknerian weavings of David Bradley to discover whether warp and woof are both verisimilitudinous. Or will he find that one direction is imagination and the other fact, that the real liar's truth is made of that combination? And will David Bradley's truth match in any way with Maxine Kumin's, in which every piece is recognizable and would be no more than a picture of life if life were as ordered as art?

Furthermore, artists are dangerous: they have theories about the world. Fortunately, there are more theories in their conversation than in their work. But after hearing about the world in theory, the editor becomes concerned. What is the connection between poverty and crime? Is there something political about a criminal act? Are the disabled, the weakest of all, really being arbitrarily dropped from the welfare rolls?* The Reagan administration is cruel, but it is not composed of beasts.

What does it mean to be a discouraged worker? How does one feel? The best way to check facts seemed to be to go out in the world and have a look, to find out if what the writers said was like a bad experiment, neither repeatable nor reproducible.

I met a man who looked like my uncle Sol. He carried the same luggage under his eyes. I am well acquainted with *The Nation,* he said, although I have not read it or any other publication for several years.

We had difficulty making conversation, for he frequently

* Several states have sued the federal government alleging that people suffering from heart disease have been improperly denied Social Security benefits. Senator William S. Cohen, of Maine, a Republican, claimed to have an internal memo from the Social Security agency instructing administrative law judges to remove 45 cases a month from the rolls. There are 780 such judges attached to the agency. If all complied, 35,000 people a month—420,000 in a single year—would lose their benefits.

dropped out to complain of the heat in the room or to stare out the window. He wished to look like a professor at some urban university, I thought, because he wore a blue beret and horn-rimmed glasses. And he would have been successful at it if he hadn't needed a shave and worn two jackets and a sweater under his coats.

His speech was cultured, New York softened by England or the South (it turned out to be both: Canada and South Carolina). He wore gentleman's boots, with a side zipper and wing tips; they would have been elegant if they had not been so badly scuffed. They were like his hands, which were large, with long, slender fingers marred by deep cuts and scabs surrounded by discolorations.

"I'm fifty-six years old," he said. "You see this white in my hair? No one wants to hire a man fifty-six years old."

He dropped out for a moment, returning only to say, "Age discrimination is illegal."

The building he lived in had burned; he had no place to sleep. He waited for the welfare department to call his name, to send him to another single-room-occupancy hotel.

He said he was not a good Muslim. Although he used the name Elijah Muhammad, he did not go to the mosque, because he did not follow the rules for proper behavior: he drank; he drank whatever he could whenever he could get it.

"I sit in the park all day," he said. "I talk to the boys. When you're on S.S.I., you're a nonperson, you're no one. You have no positive value, you're a negative value in the society. We don't vote, we're not political, because we're no one."

Liza Whitfield was getting along in 1980. Arthritis and coronary disease had left her almost immobilized, her daughter was mentally ill, her grandchildren were getting more difficult, but she was surviving with the help of day care for the children and a chore provider at home. Now, under new rules, with less money, with a different definition of disability, the welfare department in Michigan has taken away the chore provider and the day care for her grandchildren. Food stamps for the Whitfields were cut from over a hundred dollars to only fifty-seven.

Mrs. Whitfield sits in a chair to cook. She can't get around enough to keep house or manage the children. She doesn't understand the sudden decision to make life impossible for her. Meanwhile, the pressures grow inside her house. "Even now," she said, "I can feel myself letting go."

Without day care or a chore provider, the future of the Whitfield family is not difficult to predict. Liza Whitfield's daughter will be institutionalized, her grandchildren will be placed in foster homes, and Mrs. Whitfield will be left alone to sit before her stove or to move breathlessly from bed to chair and chair to bed.

Francisco Reyes is forty-two years old. He had been the owner of a small grocery store before he got a pushcart license before he became a printer. He was a union printer, working steadily until the middle of 1981. He has not worked since. The company he worked for has gone out of business. Francisco Reyes no longer has any hope of finding work.

We spoke mainly in English, with some Spanish. I have translated the Spanish, trying to keep the flavor of his speech. This is how he tells of his life now in New York City:

I grew up on a hundred and second. In those days it was good. Everybody had a job. You know Kennedy, he help poor people. Nobody need to steal, to take you watch, you ring.

Now people confused, walking like a zombie. Landlord raise the rent, where you gonna go? You can't even complain. You do things you don't even want to do.

The pressure is the thing. You don't have time to think. You can't survive. Like the walls coming closer. The pressure. You going to go up. The four walls coming closer, man, the pressure.

Now Reagan got the pressure on the poor people, not the rich people. They got to survive.

They give me a hundred and thirty dollars every fifteen days. I pay rent seventy-six dollars plus utilities. That leaves me forty-seven. I pay twenty dollars to the woman who cares for my daughter. That leaves me twenty-seven dollars for two weeks. I buy pork and beans, wait for a special. You can't buy a soda, because it costs fifty cents. You buy that, you gonna starve. That's why you feel the walls coming closer.

When I used to work, I gave the woman fifty dollars, sixty dollars. Now she does it for twenty dollars. She care for my daughter. She has feeling, you know. I appreciate it. To help my daughter I would do stealin', I would kill people, maybe they kill me.

You don't have seventy-five cents, you can't go nowhere. You have to stay on the block day after day. That's the pressure, the four walls. What happen to me? I just hang in there, see if I get a job. I know I'm not gonna do nothin' foolish, because I got a daughter. If I was by myself, I would go and stick up people, I would kill 'em. But if I go to jail, I would be dead, because I wouldn't help my daughter. If not for her, I wouldn't have nothing to lose, just my life.

Now I'm doin' WF [workfare] with sanitation to get my food stamps. They don't make me mad; what makes me mad is that Reagan is ruining people's minds. Nobody's talkin' much, just thinkin'. Everybody's talkin' short. Got problems. Everybody's thinkin', where am I gonna get a dollar to buy cigarettes, to buy a soda?

Now no jobs anywhere, only computer. You got to have college for that. Five years ago there was jobs, money was runnin'. Now everybody's walkin' like a zombie. I pray God's gonna help me, but sometimes it's not your turn. Maybe you never get your turn. It's like numbers. That's life.

You remember Hilgar [Hitler], who used to kill the Jews? Reagan's something like him, but Reagan, he uses psychology on the people. He kills people but he kills them slowly. You feel the pain day by day. He kill you.

Before '84 a lot of people going to be dead—from muggings, from robbing the wagon that brings money to the store.

A gun costs a lot now, two hundred and fifty dollars. The price went up because you get a year automatically for carrying it. It's not a big risk, not now. With the pressure, you can't even think.

My wife died in the summer. Asthma. She was twenty-six. Life changed. Company, man. When you have a friend, a real friend, and they go away, you don't have company anymore. Lonely. After my wife died I be by myself. I don't have no friends anymore. Everything changed. You don't have no friends like you did twenty years ago. People don't help you. Who's going to help you? Reagan made us all alone. You don't do nothing unless you get paid. We all alone. We killing each other, mugging each other. Reagan make us evil. He make you like him. He the fucking devil.

Good people don't make it. Only the devil get to the top. The person have a good heart, the devil find a way to get rid of him. Like Reagan, he think like a Communist; he don't care about nobody.

Two weeks ago, one jumped from the roof of my building. I went downstairs to find out why he jumped. They raised his rent. He went from $179 to $210. He only gets $150 a week for himself and his wife and two kids. He was workin' on Canal Street, doin' deliveries. When they raise his rent, he couldn't stand the pressure. You'll see, man, a lot of people kill themselves, off the roof, under the train.

The whole game is you just move around, West Side, East Side. Sooner or later, they gonna get you, but first you make some money. People confused, people not thinking. Time is short. You always got to be thinking about where to get a dollar, help somebody unload a truck, something.

My mother died in 1976. My father—I never knew him—I think he's still alive. My mother raised us. I feel like I'm gonna go up, but I keep waitin'. I want to find out what's gonna happen.

You got to keep moving, watching where you can save a few pennies. Time is short, man. You got to think.

At night, I watch the news, all the news on all the channels. Then I lay in bed thinking where am I gonna get a dollar? I don't watch nothin' on TV but the news, to see what the devil, he's going to cut next.

In the morning I go to the park to breathe, then I move around, East Side, West Side, looking for a place to make a dollar, maybe help someone fix something or load a truck, anything to make a dollar. You got to be always thinking how to make a dollar. Time is short. That's why people confused, walkin' around thinkin'. People be like zombies.

These people from other countries, they come here, they work for anything. A job be worth a hundred and fifty dollars, they do it for one hundred dollars. Don't matter. They do anything. I see on the news, Reagan sending money to El Salvador, Africa. They never pay it back. And me, I be walkin' the street like a zombie, man, because they cut me from sixty-eight dollars to forty-eight dollars.

Time is short, man.

You mug somebody. Maybe you kill somebody. You don't think about it, man. The pressure. There's no time to think. Maybe he kill you. It don't matter, man; there's no time.

Several people connected with the New York City courts told me that it was not now uncommon for people to be arrested for stealing food, which they believed was a serious symptom of the desperation caused by reductions in social programs. I was not able to verify their assertion, although I have no reason to doubt its accuracy. Sitting through hours of arraignments is far more demoralizing than talking to people at a soup kitchen. The youth of the people who have been arrested is ominous. The connection between poverty, racism, and the kinds of crimes for which people are arrested and imprisoned is blatant. One cannot assign the disasters that are exposed in the courtroom to the business cycle; the problems are fundamental; this society is failing great numbers of its members. The state of desperation, were it any other disease, would be named an epidemic.

What the writers said does not seem overstated. If anything, they have spoken softly. Ernest Hebert and Edward Rivera write of the near, intimately, almost in whispers. David Ray opens his own childhood to examine the new politics that resulted from that old Depression. Simon Ortiz sees that education is also a social program.

Much more needs to be said. But who should speak? What effect will the words have?

IV

"Once upon a time men were all things: poets, thinkers, legislators, land surveyors, musicians, warriors," said Leibniz. The young Karl Marx later pictured such a life as his ideal. We cannot remember the time when men were all things; we do not know for certain that such a time existed. If it should come again, no one would be more surprised than the specialized toilers of the late-twentieth century, this time when a person who can both read and do long division considers himself an intellectual, when the disciplines are crossed only by the brave and the foolish.

Perhaps we have been overcome by the sciences. If a mechanical engineer and a biochemist cannot trade places, how can a poet be a legislator? It is impossible, according to current beliefs, to find a philosopher among hoplites. The division of labor has boiled us down to creatures who barely fill the definition of man. Our business leaders and stuporous social scientists praise the Japanese for having found the means to almost totally integrate man into the assembly line, as if the highest aspiration of man were to labor, artlessly, at another's command.

In this narrow new world, art begins to be limited to itself. The poet, who once had as much standing in the community as the doctor, has been put into a niche with other useless things, somewhere below the hairdresser and the interior decorator. The novelist, for most people, has nothing at all to do with art: the cousins of the common pornographer have their uses, while the writers of romances and adventures help their readers pass the time between movies and situation comedies. Theories of art make little sense in this new situation: Aristotelian tragedy isn't likely; we can hardly get through a week on the bestseller list, let alone Hume's test of a classic; Tolstoy's notion of utility doesn't work any better now than it did when he wrote it; Croce doesn't offer any guidance about what ought to go along the telegraph wire; and the objective correlative takes us about as far as an *obiter dictum* can be expected to in our quest for the key to art in our time.

We drift now, like vessels capsized in the tide: the top has become the bottom and the bottom the top; what was once consigned to the private realm is now the necessity of social life, and action is left to our dreams. What shall we say? What shall we do when we are not daydreaming on the job or asleep in the grass?

A critic and novelist wrote recently that *Finnegans Wake* was definitely the last novel. The writer was standing in the doorway of old age at the time but cannot be assumed to be too old to write another novel. The statement was not a farewell; it was an act of suicide, the killing of all those who remain. Of itself the statement has little importance; it serves only to remind us that in a time of reversed realms, without a common aesthetic to knit the culture into strength, the artist lives excoriated, vulnerable to all worldly occurrences and with no possibility of being modest about his moral position.

The first problem for the novelist, as for the artist in general in such a fix, is not what to make or how to make it, but whether to make anything at all; why bother? The camera has replaced the paintbrush, most of the melodies within mathematical possibility have been written, the novel has been used up, events have replaced art. Furthermore, with the public and private realms reversed, art can only be made about the private realm (where action now takes place in freedom), and the private realm ceases to be private when it is no longer secret: art is left to deal with nowhere, to turn on itself. Why bother?

Propaganda has not been eliminated, like the novel, by having been said. Artists could become propagandists; totalitarian regimes of both the Left and the Right have found artists useful in making propaganda, although the policy of such regimes is always to kill artists for making art. Perhaps this response of assassins implies something about the nature of art; surely it proves that utility alone can be no measure of art, as gratuitousness alone does not make for art. The most important implications, it seems to me, of the totalitarian response to art have to do with the role of the artist.

The subject of art cannot be limited to the private realm, nor can works of art exist limited to the private. If ever we chance to eavesdrop on the art of the purely private, we are sure to find

that it is like the humor that provokes laughter in those gentle
lunatics who sit on the sidewalks of cities: without meaning for
anyone but the laughing lunatic. The artist, no matter how
concerned with language or form or other art, must first overcome the "why bother," then make art; the alternatives are
lunatic privacy or the nowhere between the realms.

For what purpose does one choose to make art: to do or to
make? If art is merely what doers are left to when they cannot
succeed in the world of action, it is sorry indeed. On the other
hand, if art is purely making, with the sense of permanence and
divorce from the changing world of action that pure making
implies, of what consequence can it possibly be? The artist
wishes to be the doer who does not die. Only for such a glorious
possibility do artists take the risks that leave so many ruined and
unknown, failed in both the fleeting act and the endless moment, pretenders who posed no danger to the past or the future.

Finally, it is danger as much as any other characteristic that
differentiates art from propaganda or journalism or any other
labor. That is why there can be no conservative art; the work of
artists is always profoundly revolutionary. Art cannot be forced
into the realm of the private. It exists in the public realm, like
politics. Necessity may limit public freedom, for necessity is the
most violent restraint, but even necessity cannot make politics
private or hunger secret. There is a public realm in the best and
worst of societies; there must be, for neither love nor murder
can be accomplished in complete privacy or without the freedom that permits it to occur.

Artists behave no less dangerously than lovers or assassins.
They are equally immoderate, gamblers all, people who act in
hope of immortality but never in pursuit of a gentle old age.
Whoever is not subject to arrest in the mind of some despot or
would-be despot is not an artist. There will be no art in paradise,
only propaganda to support the status quo.

V

Steinbeck, Agee, Algren, Conroy, Welty, and all the others
went bravely into the world in the nineteen thirties. They had

no wish but to be dangerous. They went to get evidence of the intolerable; they wrote to bring their readers to the world. They were optimists and rebels who never learned despair.

The writers of this book follow them. There is a new generation to bring to the world.

The works that appear in this book may be compared to sketches. There will be more. This is a sample book. The work is not done; the moment for action does not pass; the doer, who is also the maker, takes part in a profound revolution. Freedom from necessity, the ability to imagine happiness, something close enough to equality to enable everyone to hold out hope, a government for the people: we are Americans, citizens of a practical nation; we seek a modest paradise.

EARL SHORRIS

$222

ERNEST HEBERT

SHIRLEY HODGE'S WESTERN-STYLE BELT BUCKLE IS ETCHED IN purple with the words "bull shit."

I remark on the buckle, and she says, "That's how I feel about this world right now."

Shirley and I grew up together in Keene, New Hampshire, a town of about twenty-five thousand people and the hub and service center for twenty thousand more spread out in small villages in the southwestern part of the state. Keene rests on the flat of an ancient lake bed between pretty, wooded hills. Winter is cold and snowy, summer warm and pleasant, fall brief and colorful, spring almost nonexistent.

Shirley lives with her mother, Lillian Hodge, now ninety-two, in a small four-room apartment on the corner of Church and Carpenter streets, in Keene. The apartment is on the second floor of a three-story, wood-frame house that has seen better days. The rent is seventy dollars a week. Shirley likes the place, mainly because the landlord, Arnold Patnaude, keeps it nice and warm in the winter and takes care of any problems with the building. "Arnold's all right—decent," says Shirley.

She is wearing her standard Shirley Hodge uniform: dark slacks, Western shirt and Western belt, from which dangles a rabbit's foot. Her short dark hair is graying; she's much too heavy for good health. She has no teeth.

"The teeth were removed, oh, three years ago," she says. "They were just too far gone to do me any good. I have to eat hamburg or hot dogs, soup, things like that, something soft that I don't have to chew. I take and cut up my food real fine. I eat things that are good for me too, like oranges and applesauce. I am supposed to be on a strict diet because of my diabetes, and I give myself the insulin, but I haven't had the cash to buy the things I should for the diet. Maybe I could be better at it. Sure, I'd like to get some false teeth, but I can get by without teeth. It's more important to fix my car (a rusted, 1975 Ford Maverick) when it's broke, because if I can't get to the store there'd be no food for my mother and me to eat. See, with my leg the way it is, I need a car. I need the car for work, too. I mean, I'm not working but I need it to look for work."

We walk into the living room. It's neat and homey. On the walls are romanticized pictures of animals.

"Yah, I'm crazy about animals, especially horses," Shirley says, and points to a black velvet painting of a stallion rearing up on his hind legs. "That one is my pride and joy. I bought it at Woolworth's."

The most unusual object in the room is a teddy bear big as a man, sitting in a chair holding two smaller bears.

Shirley shows me a polaroid picture that reveals a likeness of E.T.

"It's a picture of a cake for my fiftieth birthday," Shirley says. "My neighbor upstairs was kind enough to bake it. She knows I like E.T. I don't usually go to movies any more, but my girlfriend's sister had said that she had gone and seen it and that we should go. I kinda hesitated, but my girlfriend kept after me— 'Can we go? Can we go?'—so I says okay. Boy, I'm not sorry we went. If more people could have a friend like E.T., why, what a better world this would be!"

Shirley and I reminisce about old times on Oak Street, where we grew up, and she answers my questions readily enough, but in fact she's preoccupied with her troubles. Two days ago she had a knee operation. She also has another leg injury that can't be corrected, and she's often in pain. Sometimes she can walk all right, but at other times she needs a cane or crutches to get around. The injury is the result of an on-the-job accident in 1979. In addition, she was laid off recently from her job as a factory worker, and her worker's compensation benefits are almost exhausted. According to her reckoning, she's got two weeks of benefits due, but after talking to an official at the State Office of Employment Security, she doubts whether she will get the money. It's only $222, but after that, the only income in the Hodge household is her mother's small welfare check, not nearly enough to pay the rent and buy food. She's expecting a letter from the employment office informing her of whether she's eligible for two more weeks of benefits. There's more than just the money involved. There's anger that she's going to be screwed by officialdom; there's fear that she doesn't have the resources to provide for herself. My first memory of Shirley is of her bringing an armload of firewood into the kitchen of the Hodges' four-room apartment at 11 Oak Street. She was a ruggedly built tomboy with dark hair and plain features, eight years older than I. My family lived next door, at 19 Oak Street.

I liked hanging around the Hodge place. The kitchen had a nice smell, of pies and radiant heat and something else from the outdoors, an essence, from snow brought in with the firewood that had melted and picked up the scent of trees and released it into the air. Nobody else in our neighborhood burned wood. These were the days before wood-burning chic had swept into the New England states. Heating oil was cheap and plentiful— statusy, too. People who burned wood were considered old-fashioned, eccentric, or poor, but I didn't know that at the time. I was five years old, and I thought wood heat quite exotic.

I felt comfortable and safe in Shirley's presence. All the neighborhood children did. Shirley had a temper, but she directed it laterally against peers or upward against adults such as school officials; never downward. With kids, cats, puppies, bowl fish, anything weaker than herself, she was kind and gentle. She gave a kid the feeling that she had assigned herself as his protector.

Shirley's father died the year she was born. She has a brother and a sister who were grown and on their own by the time I met her, and another brother several years older than herself, named Donald, who was in and out of the household. When Donald was around, Shirley became wary and especially protective of the weaker creatures in the neighborhood. Donald was a young man full of rage and inner hurt. Once, when we children found a pigeon with a broken wing, Donald picked up the bird, eyed it for a moment, then hurled it against a stone wall—"to put it out of his misery," he said. Another time, he became angry at a used car he had bought and destroyed it with a sledgehammer.

Oak Street connects Beaver Street and Roxbury Street. It's built into the side of Beech Hill, with six modest wood-frame houses about fifty feet apart along the upper side of the street. The East Side of Keene includes a dotting of nice houses occupied by upper-middle-class people. There are also a number of houses which have been chopped up into cramped apartments and let to students, other young people, and poor families, but basically it's a working-class neighborhood of single-family houses, not much different now than when Shirley and I were growing up. The kids still play touch football on the street; they still play chase games along the hill in back. The main difference is there are fewer elm trees and more cars parked in the yards.

The Clappers, Shirley's aunt and uncle, rented the upstairs apartment at 11 Oak Street. Hiram Clapper raised chickens in a coop cut into the side of the hill, and he planted several small gardens on the property. He also kept bees, which Shirley sometimes helped him tend. The Clappers and the Hodges came from country stock, and today Shirley talks about how nice it would be to live on a farm. The Clappers are both dead now, and Shirley doesn't know where Donald is. She still keeps in touch with her older brother and sister, who live in the Keene area.

Shirley's mother, Lillian Hodge, scraped out a marginal living taking in washing and ironing. She also made quilts and fancy embroidery. They fetched a fair price, but they took a long time to make. Lillian Hodge continued this work until she had to stop because of poor eyesight and trembling hands. The embroidery remains a badge of Hodge pride.

"Some of the things my mother made were so beautiful that we hated to sell them," Shirley says. "I tried to learn the work, but I just didn't have the talent for it."

Shirley was not a good student in school; she never got beyond the tenth grade. And today, although she has no trouble grasping ideas and she has been a lifelong reader (she rarely watches television), there's an intellectual blind spot in her fitness IQ for survival in our times, our country. The fine points of grammar and social nicety, the ability to cultivate relationships for gain, a sensitivity to the prevailing fashions in dress and opinion, a nose for the wind that helps one know when to tack in the workaday seas—these have escaped her. Furthermore, although she is a good person who neither drinks nor smokes, she lacks much of what gives a woman standing in the community. She is not rich, not slim, not pretty, not elegant, not hip, not toothy, not married, not connected. Her lines were formed early: She knew she was destined for shopwork; she knew it was going to be her lot in life to take care of her mother in her old age.

"I would have liked to have finished high school, knowing what I know now: They don't want you in this town unless you've got the education," she says. "But when I was sixteen, I felt like I had to take and get a job to help my mother. So I quit school. I've been working ever since; I mean, when I haven't been laid off. You can say this for me: I never been fired from a job. I've been laid off time and again, and out of work, and I know what it's like to go down there to sign up for unemployment, but I never been fired. Some people go back to school, and I've thought about getting more education, but I don't think I could concentrate, because I'd be, ah, worrying about things, and my memory's not too good. I write everything down, names, dates. I can't remember 'em, but I can find 'em.

"Yes, I guess you can say I'm organized. When I'm out of work, I read the want ads real close, and I pound the streets looking for work. I go down regular to the unemployment office, and I'll say this, they've been good down there, except for this gentleman I talked to yesterday who it looks like won't give me the two weeks' benefits I got coming. But listen, they didn't find the jobs for me. I found my own jobs.

"My first job was working at Keene Steam Laundry for fifty cents an hour, which was on Church Street. It's long gone. I had just turned sixteen, which was the minimum age where you could take a job. I worked on what they call a mangle. I must have been there, oh, a whole year before I was laid off. Then I went to the New Hampshire chair company, in South Keene. I done everything down there. I worked on the saws and sanders, mostly on sanders. And then I worked on what they call a planer. That takes the bark and stuff all off the wood. And I sanded the chairs, the seats and all. I think that job lasted over a year, but I lost it when they went out of business. And then I went up to Marlow [fifteen miles north of Keene]. They had a wood-product company up there, making bookcases and tool chests for the Army. I had worked up there two weeks and my boss told me on a Friday that I was going to get a raise the following week because I was doing such a good job and—wouldn't you know it—the place burned down."

Shirley then landed a job at a small shop that made costume jewelry. She was nineteen years old.

"It was mostly foot-press work over there," she says. "They used to make bracelets, cuff links and earrings—you know, pierced ears? the wires? I ran a machine that made these things for cuff links, looked like bullets. They had two machines that was side by side. You put the pieces in and then you took 'em out. The machine was alone with you. I mean you could stop anytime you wanted to, and it wasn't like a line, that makes you keep up no matter whether you can or can't. It was mostly setting-down work. I liked it."

Shirley worked in the shop for twenty-one years—good years, perhaps her best years. Her personality as an adult emerged. She developed a small circle of friends; she was especially close to Dorothy Wicks, whose picture is on the living-room wall beside her nephew's. She kept her dark hair cut short and used no makeup. She developed a look that was all her own for a woman in a small New England city: blue jeans or slacks, Western shirt, Western belt and buckle, attached to the belt a rabbit's foot and a folding knife in a case.

"I like the West," she says. "I got interested in it from, well, back when they had those movies—Roy Rogers and Gene Autry and Hopalong Cassidy and another one that I can't think of right now. Back then, in the Old West, living was hard, but people were more friendly. You could get to know 'em, and they wouldn't ask you a lot of questions. They went by day-to-day things. They didn't dig in the past, and see how you lived or whether one of your relatives might be the black sheep of the family. That kind of thing. I'd sure like to go there, to the West. I've always seen movies of it, and I'd like to go there, to the Rockies, the Grand Canyon. It would be really something to see. But I never had the money to do that much traveling. Oh, I thought about it years ago when I was healthy and my car was running good, yes I did, but I kinda didn't want to go alone."

The house at 11 Oak Street was sold when Shirley was in her early twenties, and she and her mother had to leave. They found a place on Church Street, in Keene. Shirley had a small apartment upstairs, and her mother a room downstairs. There was a plot for a garden so Lillian could plant flowers, but the house itself was inferior to the one on Oak Street. There was no wood stove, and the landlord controlled the heat. The rooms were cold in the winter and hot in the summer, Shirley says. Later, the house was condemned by the city inspector as unfit for habitation and torn down. The Hodges moved next door. That house, too, eventually was condemned. The two women then moved into Arnold Patnaude's apartment house. He is a good landlord, as opposed to bad landlords. The Hodges' peace of mind depends largely on the goodness of landlords, especially since the apartments the Hodges are likely to rent, those they can afford, tend to be rundown and require frequent repairs.

Shirley has never lived in a house that she owned. Ask her whether she'd like to buy a house, and she struggles to answer. She'd like a place in the country, a farm or a ranch, she says, then confesses that she has never allowed herself to dream about such things. There was never enough money, or even the possibility of money, to make a dream of owning a house more than a frustrating tease. In the twenty-one years she worked at the jewelry shop, her pay hovered around the minimum wage. A full-time job was a just-getting-by living.

There are few union shops in the Keene area, and in general, workers are not paid much. However, up until recently, when unemployment climbed to 10 percent, there has been plenty of work. Since wages are low and living costs high, it usually takes a household two wage earners to support a mortgage and modern amenities. In a Keene working-class family, the man works one or two jobs; the woman works one job, takes care of the kids and does the housework. A newly married couple, even if they both work, usually require a financial boost from family to get started buying their own home. For single people without family money, for one-income householders supporting one or more additional persons, it's only those who make very good money or have the entrepreneurial gift who can afford to buy a house in Keene. A steady job is not enough.

Another issue affecting people, like Shirley, with marginal incomes is the automobile. It used to be that you could get by without a car in Keene. Buses ran the major arteries and carried people to the industrial park, where most of the factories were. There were handy markets on every street corner. It was not only the iceman that cometh, but the milkman and the grocer and a host of other vendors. You could phone in your food order, as my own mother did, and the grocer delivered the food. It was nice to have a car, but it wasn't necessary. That's all changed now. There's a "friendly bus" for the old folks, but no regular line to serve people going to and from work. Small stores are zoned out of neighborhoods. About the only thing you can get delivered to your house is pizza. Like everywhere else, Keene is geared for the motorist. Food, shelter, work, a car—these are the basics for survival today in Keene, New Hampshire.

"When I was working and there was some extra money, it went for a movie and maybe to go out to eat once in a while, and anyway there would be never enough to make a down payment on a house, because it had to go for the cars that I owned—used cars; I never bought a new car. I'd have to take and pay out because things would go wrong with them. I did that to tires and, like, oil changes and grease jobs; there was batteries I had to buy, plugs I had to get, fuel pumps. You know, just one goldarn thing after another. Sometimes I didn't have a car at all, and that's hard, because everything you need is so far away today. I didn't mind so much, you know—walking—back before my leg was hurt. But now, why I would not want to have to walk everywhere. I might be able to manage, maybe, in the summer. In winter, I just couldn't do it."

Life took a turn for the worse for Shirley when she was laid off, quite suddenly, from the jewelry shop.

"I worked there for twenty-one years, and I thought I'd work there forever, because it was steady, a job I could count on even if it didn't pay too good," Shirley says. "I guess business got kind of slow and they laid off all the ones that had worked there like me—for twenty-one years, nineteen years, twenty years, and so on. The week after that, we heard they had hired all new people in there, young ones. There was two or three of us that went down to the unemployment office to see if anything could be done, but there couldn't. The guy in there that we talked to said a shop doesn't have to keep the old ones if they don't want to, and there's no law that says they have to hire you back. I knew then, that was the end of that."

Shirley is well organized when it comes to filing records of her misfortunes. She has folders full of such things as reminders of doctors' appointments, medical records and layoff notices. No doubt that letter she's expecting from the employment office regarding her two weeks in benefits will end up in one of the folders. Using her papers as reminders, she recounts her work life since the layoff at the jewelry shop and the accident several years later that has made life more difficult.

"When they laid me off at the jewelry shop, that's when things started to go bad," she says. "First off, I hit the road looking for work. And I did get a job at Roberts-Hart [a shoe shop], but then I heard of an opening at MPB [a modern, miniature ball-bearing plant], and I decided to apply. I wanted to better myself. I kinda hesitated, because I didn't think I could pass the test, but I passed and got the job. That was October 14, 1974. They started me off at more than I was making at Roberts-Hart or that I had made in all those years at the jewelry shop. I was surprised. I'd never seen good money like that before. I can't remember exactly how much it was, but it was over two dollars an hour. I wasn't there long—six months—when I heard a rumor there was going to be a layoff, and sure enough sixty of us got laid off.

"I went down and signed up for unemployment, and I was out of work six weeks when I got a job at Keene Wood Heel, down there on Water Street. I was a sander and I worked all kinds of saws, handled lumber and everything. We was equal with the men there. If we didn't like the job we was doing we could quit. I even worked unloading boxcars. That job lasted about a year and I got laid off.

"I heard of an opening at MPB, so I went there and they hired me back. I liked it there. I liked the people and the work was all right and the money was good. And then I got hurt. It was May

26, 1977. I slipped on that oil and I pulled the adductor muscle here in my thigh, and I've had all kinds of trouble since then. I had an oilcan in my hand, to go around the back of the machine to put oil in and, ah, I didn't see this oil on the floor and my heel hit it, I slipped, and all my weight went on the oilcan and I kind of threw myself back. When I did, I heard this popping sound, sounded like it came from the front of me somewhere. I knew I had done something. And it was five or ten minutes after that that I begin to get that awful pain. I could hardly walk. I went to the doctor the next day, and they took X rays and everything, and it didn't show anything that was broke. He said I had pulled that adductor muscle. I've got this all written down. There it is, a-d-d-u-c-t-o-r m-u-s-c-l-e."

Since the accident, Shirley has never quite felt right. The pains in her leg come and go. She has worked at MPB only off and on, sometimes leaving because her leg was bothering her, sometimes because she's been laid off. Physical injuries aside, she seems to have lost heart. She's preoccupied with her folders, as if therein lies the meaning of her life.

"It was April 17, 1979, when I had to leave work because that leg was giving me so much trouble," she says. "There was a lot of doctors that I saw. I've been up to Hanover and I went to Boston for a CAT scan down there. There was fourteen doctors in all that I seen. They all told me the same thing: I was going to be bothered with it for the rest of my life. There was things they could do, but there wasn't any guarantee that things may help.

"This operation I had this week was to see what was causing the knee to go out on me, because I'd be walking along and it would feel, you know, like it hit you in the back of the knee. Remember when we was kids and we'd come up and hit you in the back of the knee? Well, that's what it would be like if you had what I had. I can't read what the operation is called. It's a great big long word. The doctor told me that he went in there and cleaned it all up. He said it looked pretty good. I gotta go back next week to see him again. There's no guarantee, and it's not going to help above here, where the main pull is. This is just to see if they can stop that knee from giving out."

I suggest vaguely that Shirley might consider signing on to some retraining program to learn a trade in which she wouldn't be on her feet. But she doesn't have the confidence to imagine herself anywhere but in a shop. The future seems dismal, and she doesn't even like to think about it. What are your hopes? I ask.

"Right now it's really hard to say what I hope for," she says. "You really can't plan on nothing, the way the work is. I haven't had any learning to do, ah, secretarial work or anything like that. I don't know."

Just to get her to talk about something else besides her troubles, I ask her what she would do if somebody gave her a million dollars. She laughs, surprised at the question.

"Jeez, I don't know," she says. "I never thought of anything like that before. Let me think . . . ah, I think I, I ah, would take and put it away, to have something to go back on when I got older."

I press on, insisting that if she were to accept the gift she'd have to spend a healthy chunk of the money.

"Well, maybe I'd take that trip out West and see out and around through there," she says.

Then it's back to talking about what's really on her mind: the encounter she had with the man at the employment office the day after her operation.

"The last time I worked was February 25 of this year [1983], when they laid me off," she says. "I thought it was going to be longer, but the orders had slowed down so they had to take and (I guess) close down some parts of the shop, and then they had to put their other help—you know, that's been there longer than I have—back onto the floor. They told me just as quick as things picked up they'd call us back, but right now I can't work anyway because on account of that operation I had.

"When I was laid off last April [of 1982] I could draw unemployment out of my twenty-six weeks. And then I used that up and they had extended it for another six weeks. And I had used that up, and then they had called me back down at the shop December 20. So, I had two more weeks coming to me on that extended weeks that they get that they had given us. Then I found out I had to have this operation. Well, it was supposed to have been in January, but I postponed it because I thought I was going to be able to work. I wanted to see how I'd get along, doing this job. It was hard, but it was setting down most of the time. I didn't have too much walking to do. But then they laid me off anyway, so I decided to get the operation.

"But I was looking for a job, too. I had gone down to the unemployment office February the twenty-eighth and signed up. And I had to go in the month of March to sign up again. And I had been all over Keene, you know, looking for work. There's just nothing available. So I was to go back to the unemployment office the sixteenth. I got out of the hospital and had a friend of mine come and get me because I couldn't drive anyway. And I had my papers that I was to take down there and see if I could draw those two weeks of unemployment that they owed me.

"Now, I don't know whether I should take and tell the gentleman's name or not who gave me all the trouble. I talked with Mr. XXXXX down there. I guess he's the head one. He, ah, wanted to, ah, know what this is all about and all the operation and things. I said this was on account of the accident that I had down to MPB. And I wanted to take and sign up for the two weeks in March. He says, You wasn't willing and able to work, was you? And I says, Yes. (Raises her voice in indignation.) I didn't go in the hospital, I says, until the fifteenth, to have my operation. I was looking all along before that for work. He says, I don't think that you'll be able to get anything. I says, I can talk to my lawyer about it. He says, You go right ahead; it's my decision to make. If I don't want to pay you and if I don't think that you're eligible for it, I don't have to pay you. He was really snotty.

"I had been down there since twenty-five minutes of two, and I never got out of there until quarter past three, waiting, you know, talking with him and he had gone through my files and everything. And I says to this gentleman, I can go to my doctor. He says, You do that. You tell him that I want a statement from him telling that you was willing and available for work for those two weeks in March. I went back up the clinic—that's where doctor Hansen has his office—and I talked to his nurse, and I told him what I wanted, you know what I needed from doctor Hansen. And I felt kind of bad. I broke down and started to cry. I had just got out of the hospital and have him—the gentleman —you know, say that. Because they take and give you a paper and on it you have to take and put down all the places that you go to and the people that you talk to. All that was all written on this paper, that I had gone looking for a job for the first week in March and the second week in March. So, anyway, Dr. Hansen's nurse, he took and—it's a male, Fred—he said that he would talk to Dr. Hansen and he'd take and send it out. So, yesterday, I, ah, went down to MPB and talked to the personnel director about what had happened down at the unemployment office. She said that if I got a letter denying those two weeks, for me to appeal it, because she says you were willing and available for work. She says because if we had the work you wouldn't have ever got laid off, you'd a been working. But I still haven't got nothing from him yet."

The next day I telephone Shirley to ask how things are going. Her voice manages to convey both anger and fear. She'd gotten the letter from the employment office. I ask her to read it. Calmed somewhat by the concentration of having to read over the telephone, she says:

" 'The Federal Supplementary Compensation Act has been amended and now provides New Hampshire claimants additional entitlement of two times their weekly benefit rates. Your maximum remaining entitlement is $222. This decision serves only to increase your potential maximum benefit amount. Any disqualification in effect for not meeting this eligibility requirement remains in effect.' So, see, see what he's saying?"

I don't see. The jargon boggles my mind. Shirley explains, "What he's saying is: I'm not eligible for it."

Segundo's Benefits

EDWARD RIVERA

THE TROUBLE STARTED ONE MORNING IN MAY, WHEN Segundo lost his balance and fell in the passage between the bedroom and the bathroom. He got back up, he wasn't hurt, but he felt dizzy and his head was overheated. He thought he might be coming down with a virus, but decided against going back to bed. Whatever the trouble was, he hoped it would go away before the day was out.

When he started shaving, his sideburns were out of focus in the bathroom mirror. In fact, both sides of his face were out of focus, no matter how many times he tilted his head left and right or leaned forward. At one point he nicked the tip of his right ear. He finished shaving by holding the razor with both hands. It looked as though he was going to get to work late, so he skipped his shower, a first for him and not a very good way to start off the morning. A bad-luck sign, maybe. But he hated getting to work late.

Later, almost fifteen minutes behind, he told his wife, Magda, about it in the kitchen—about falling and feeling a little dizzy, about the high temperature in his head, about nicking his ear— and wanted to know what she thought. She took a good look at his eyes (they were watery) and said it looked to her like an eye cold. "You should go back to bed," she said. Maybe he should go see Dr. Murillo, an eye specialist on the Grand Concourse. Segundo said he'd rather wait and see. If he didn't feel better by tomorrow morning, he'd go see the eye doctor. Today he was going in to work. Just before he left, Magda squeezed a couple of Murine drops into his eyes, and while she had him in that passive, head-tilted position, she said he should come back home by noon if he didn't feel better. He said he would, and left.

By the time he got to the factory, it was already 9:05; he was thirty-five minutes late. His first lateness since 1978, the year he started working for Bob and Roy, the brothers who owned Renowned Frocks. And the reason for his lateness was that it had been a slow, tricky walk from his building on Bruckner Boulevard to the subway station on Simpson Street, then an even trickier walk from Times Square to the factory, five blocks away. Pedestrians and traffic on either side of him had looked ghostly. Every time he started crossing a street, the buzzing ghosts of cars, trucks, and buses were coming straight for him, even though he had the WALK light every time. No driver even came close to running him down, but he thought that was because he'd been so cautious. And the price he paid for that caution was his first lateness in two years.

But the truth wasn't what he told his two bosses when he apologized for being late. He told them the train he'd been on had broken down up in the Bronx; the passengers had had to get off and wait for another train, which took a long time getting there, because first the subway workmen had to switch the disabled train out of the station and onto a different track, so a "healthy" train could take over. Not an easy operation, as Bob and Roy could imagine. They said they did.

A part of him wished he had told them the truth, because this broken-down subway story was beginning to sound like a broken-down lie, but it was too late to take it back. He had a couple of reasons for keeping the truth to himself: he didn't like to discuss his personal problems on the job, and he didn't want to receive special treatment from anyone, as if he were a feeble old man already.

Roy, the younger brother, had a good sense of humor. He said Segundo's subway story reminded him of that old song about the man who got lost in the Boston subway system and was never heard from again. He sang the refrain for Segundo: "And you know he'll never return." Segundo smiled along with his bosses even though he'd never heard the song. Then Roy and Bob went back to the showroom, where there were customers waiting, and Segundo went into the shipping room, feeling slightly disoriented and slightly foolish.

His two assistants, a couple of teenagers who did not like the job, noticed his slowness right away, and his unusual silence, and ribbed him about it. Those two could be cruel when they got going on somebody. They asked him whether he was getting old or something. Of course, they had no idea what the trouble was, and he had no intention of telling them. He wasn't exactly on intimate terms with them.

"Time to retire, Seggie," the taller one of them told him.

A long time ago he had asked them not to call him by that nickname. It was silly and insulting, he said. He reminded them —as if he had to—that his correct name was Segundo, but that was a mistake: They began referring to him as "Mr. Segundo" in mock-respectful voices. And when they got tired of that nickname, they began calling him "Mr. Primero" in the same tone of voice. He had to ignore them. It was bad for his nerves and blood pressure. The trouble with these two helpers of his was that they seemed to have no respect for anyone or anything, including the work they did—not very well—for a living.

That wasn't his problem. He had nothing against his job. On the contrary, he enjoyed it. He took pride in his skills as a head shipping clerk. Roy and Bob and his previous employers, two old men for whom he'd worked a total of twenty-seven years, had never said anything bad about his work or his attitude. Just the opposite: they had always told him, and told others in his presence, that he was one of the best shipping clerks they'd ever had the privilege to hire, a real pro. And they didn't just praise him: They put their money where their mouths were. Every year he got a raise in his wages to keep him up with the cost of living. The raises usually came to five dollars, beginning the first week in January, but a couple of times, when business was booming, they gave him ten dollars. So that over the past thirty years his earnings had gone up to two hundred dollars a week, and that didn't even include the hundred dollar bonus he got every Christmas. Not bad for someone who had never even gone to high school.

He hadn't been able to. In the mountain village in Puerto Rico where he spent the first twenty years of his life, there was no such thing as a secondary school when he was a boy. And besides, being orphaned at the age of eight, he'd had to go work as an all-purpose field hand for local farmers as soon as he finished grammar school. By the time he arrived in New York, it was a little late to be starting high school, even if he had known any English, which of course he didn't. It took him years to speak it adequately, and even so, he spoke it only when he had to. It put him at a disadvantage with people whose first language was English, like those two assistants of his, with their superior posture.

He had tried talking them into joining the union, because that would make them eligible for a retirement pension and other benefits, but they had laughed off his suggestion. They said they had no intention of spending the rest of their working lives in what they called "the garment racket"; they would stay at Renowned Frocks no longer than it took to find better work. They didn't even have high school diplomas, and they were talking as if they had graduated from Columbia University or something. He wished them luck, and meant it, and said nothing more about it.

He had joined the union pension plan a long time ago, and he expected to collect something when he retired. And there was the Social Security plan, which, with careful budgeting (and he was good at that), would help keep him and Magda secure for the rest of their lives. He had nothing to complain about, and didn't, though he did regret that the two old men for whom he'd worked twenty-seven years had retired and closed down their factory.

They had always told him they'd take care of him, by which he understood that they would give him a parting bonus, a kind of unofficial pension, something off the books, when they retired. But then business started turning bad for them, partly because of a slump in the garment business and partly because they had lost interest in the trade and had not kept up with trends.

"Their fashions were going out of fashion," Segundo says, "and their business was going out of business. They were going to retire, and I was going to go out of a job."

When they did retire, in 1978, they told him they just couldn't afford to take care of him. They couldn't even afford to give him any severance pay, and hoped he understood their situation. He said he did. What they could do for him, they did.

They talked to Roy and Bob, of Renowned Frocks. Roy and Bob's own loft was upstairs in the same building. The two older men put in a good word for Segundo, praised his skills and attitude to the skies, and within a month, when Bob and Roy's head shipping clerk quit or retired ("or disappeared in the subway system," Segundo speculates), Roy called Segundo at home and told him he had himself a job if he wanted it. Same type of work, same hours and days, same pay.

Segundo certainly did want it. He had been visiting employment agencies in the Times Square area for over a month, but he'd had no luck. All the factories he visited offered him inferior jobs for inferior pay, or a job like his old one for inferior pay. He decided to hold out a little longer, collecting unemployment benefits in the meantime and taking money out of his small savings account.

If there was any money left in the bank by the time he was sixty years of age or so, it would go into his and Magda's retirement. They were thinking of going back to Puerto Rico someday (they just couldn't see themselves living out their old age in New York), after their son and daughter got on their own. Magda's late mother had left her a small plot of land in her family's hometown on the southeastern coast of the island. And Segundo and Magda planned to build themselves a small house on that plot. He still remembered a thing or two about farming, and maybe he could do a little planting and sowing when he and Magda retired. It would keep him busy, and it would save them a little money on food. It might even bring them a little income.

But that was still at least ten years off, and he and Magda saw no sense in talking about it. In the meantime, he was still putting in six days a week as Renowned Frocks' head shipping clerk, and feeling pretty secure and satisfied with his two new bosses, and vice versa. Roy and Bob certainly had not regretted hiring Segundo. Not for a minute. The man could just about run the factory all by himself, and pretty much did during the two or three weeks when they went on their summer vacation to Europe or the Caribbean or Miami Beach. The only problem was that when Segundo himself went on his summer vacation, the shipping room just about went to the dogs, because those two packing clerks of theirs just didn't have whatever it took to do a decent job. They were, frankly, one pair of fuckups, always complaining about lousy wages and shitty working conditions and never doing a thing to earn better pay. And Bob and Roy didn't have the heart to get rid of them; not yet, anyway. One of these days—just keep it up, boys.

"Without you," his bosses told Segundo, "we'd go out of business before the fiscal year's out. We'd be on the unemployment line." They might have been exaggerating a little, but he saw their point, and appreciated it.

One summer, when he was home on vacation repainting his apartment, Roy called him up to request a special favor: would he cut his vacation short one week? Because those two assistants were making such a fucking mess of things in the shipping room that Renowned Frocks was in danger of losing two of its best customers, not to mention a handful of lesser customers. The two assistant fuckups had made just about every mistake in the book. They had filled out wrong orders, mixed up others, misaddressed several top-priority shipments, and misspelled, on cartons *and* bills of lading, the names of some pretty important clients, who of course had threatened to take their business elsewhere. And who could blame them? And not only that, but those two asshole assistants were so slow that the only decent thing Roy and Bob could compare them to was a couple of slow-ass snails tied end to end.

Roy sounded desperate. He promised Segundo a nice raise at the end of the fiscal year, plus a bigger Christmas bonus, and even implied that he and his older brother were thinking of cutting Segundo in on a system called "profit-sharing." He also promised Segundo an extra week's vacation the next time business slowed down a little, during the slack season. All Segundo had to do was cut his vacation short one week.

Segundo sympathized; he put his paint and brushes back in the kitchen closet and went back to work the next day. In a couple of days he straightened everything out for Bob and Roy. While he was at it, he couldn't help telling his two assistants a thing or two about getting on the ball. Next time they messed things up, he told them, the bosses might not be so patient and lenient. The two young packers promised to get on the ball and stay on it. And they kept their word, for a few days. Then they

went back to slacking off and calling Segundo more dumb nick-
names. Segundo gave up; he ignored them and decided to let
time and things take their course.

For some reason, he never did get that extra week's vacation
he had coming to him. He guessed Roy and Bob had forgotten
about it, even when the slack season set in. It was just as well, he
decided, because what would he do with himself during that
extra week? Paint his apartment again? The idleness was bad
enough during his regular vacation. He liked working six days a
week; it brought in a few extra dollars and it kept his blood
pressure down. One thing he couldn't take too well was hanging around the house all day, getting in Magda's way, watching
TV during daylight hours, playing dominoes with himself or
with Magda (when she wasn't working herself), or with her
nephew, his best friend, Moncho, a well-paid garment cutter
down on West Thirty-seventh Street, who also didn't like taking
Saturdays off.

Sunday was the only day Segundo didn't mind loafing a little.
On the Lord's Day, he and Magda, and sometimes Moncho,
went to Mass together. All three received Communion, then
returned to Segundo and Magda's apartment for a fast-breaking
brunch. It wasn't necessary any more to fast before receiving
the host, but he and Magda, and Moncho—when he felt like it—
still liked to receive on an empty stomach. It was an old habit,
like not eating meat on Fridays, and they weren't all that interested in bringing themselves up to date on certain religious
practices as long as they had a choice. But they weren't rigid
about it. They could adjust to some innovations after a short
period of practice. They no longer minded shaking hands with
complete strangers in their pew when the Mass was over, even
though they didn't see any great spiritual benefits in that gesture. But drinking the blood of Christ, instead of just ingesting
His flesh—that was another matter. The blood might get them
high on empty stomachs, and they might stagger out of church,
making fools of themselves. They had seen others do just that.
Moncho was one of them. He was the one who looked forward
to drinking what he called, half kidding, "the bottled blood of
Our Lord. And if that's called a sacrilege," he'd add, "then I
must be in the wrong religion. Amen."

But then, Moncho was some kind of fish: a problem sometimes. All those cans of Miller and Budweiser, which he said he needed to "kill the pain," could pile up sometimes. But he could afford the stuff; he was a skilled cutter for Progressive Frocks.

During the warm time of year, Segundo and Magda went on picnics about three Sundays a month in a feeble Oldsmobile that he had bought back in 1974 for $250. Except for the TV, it was their only luxury. Five nights a week, he drove it to the subway station on East Tremont to pick up his daughter, Melida. He waited for her in the car under the elevated tracks. She worked part-time at the Gimbels near Macy's. A half hour later, the car was parked again near his building, until the same time the following night.

Almost the only other times he drove the car were when he and Magda went on those Sunday picnics to Taconic State Park, near Connecticut. Their usual companions were Moncho, his wife, Demetria, and their five-year-old son, Reynaldo. There were plenty of tables for picnickers in that park; there were lots of clean, open spaces and shade, and a pretty big, clean lake for swimming and rowing. Rowing around the lake for an hour or more was part of their picnic routine, and Moncho did most of the rowing. He was taller and considerably stronger than Segundo. During his first couple of years in New York he had, as he put it, "studied" to become a professional wrestler, the kind you see on TV. But when he met Demetria, who didn't like brutal sports, he gave up his wrestler's ambition and settled down to a gainful job in a garment factory. Now, outside of his job, he had few outlets for his excessive physical energy.

Which was why he liked to do all the rowing on that park lake, for an hour at least, without stopping to rest and letting Segundo relieve him. Segundo didn't mind it one bit. In fact, he was glad of it. He could sit back and relax, he and the others, and let Moncho work up a healthy sweat.

Another pastime on picnic Sunday was softball. Two-man softball, because their wives didn't like to participate in what they called "rough games." They both said that was for men and boys. Sometimes, frankly, it was hard to tell the difference, when you sat back and watched two grown men going at it. It was as if they regressed to boyhood as soon as they picked up the bat and the ball and put on the glove. Segundo and Moncho took turns swatting a cantaloupe-sized softball around in a clearing surrounded by trees and bushes. By the time they got done blasting the ball, it needed restitching.

"It's a good thing that ball isn't somebody's head," Magda and Demetria used to say, "or you'd both be sentenced to capital punishment."

For obvious reasons, Moncho could hit the ball much harder and farther than Segundo. He often hit it deep into the woods or out to the far end of the lake: "out of the ball park," that was called. A number of times, Segundo, the fielder, couldn't find the ball in the bushes, and Moncho and Reynaldo joined in the search; and if they couldn't find it, the two grown men would go back to the picnic table and play dominoes with their wives until it was time to drive back to Bruckner Boulevard, just before the highways clogged up with other returning picnickers and people going back home from the suburbs.

Otherwise, Segundo and Magda seldom went anywhere special. They were indifferent to movies, which were overpriced and usually boring and dishonest. The endings were hard, if not impossible, to believe: exaggerated happy endings, with everything coming out perfectly pretty for everyone, except the hissing, groaning audience; and the equally unearned unhappy endings, which left one with a bad taste in the mouth and a mild case of gloom and pessimism for the rest of the day.

Three or four times a year, they drove up to New Rochelle to see his younger sister and her husband, a retired auto mechanic. Sometimes they visited one of their neighbors in the building to play a few hands of dominoes or just to chat while the TV or the radio was playing at low volume. Wednesday evenings they both went to the weekly prayer meeting at their parish church, less than a mile away. Nowadays they had to drive there, because the streets were becoming dangerous, day and night. But if Moncho was with them and the weather was good, they walked to church. With Moncho alongside, they had nothing to worry about. Nobody was going to mess with Moncho. Except he didn't always go with them. It depended on his mood. He had a gloomy streak that would break out all of a sudden, and he'd stay home, sipping beer and watching TV, or playing with little Reynaldo.

The Wednesday meetings were run by a priest from Spain who was very serious and strict and outspoken. He would give the group of fathers and mothers little sermons (sometimes he gave them tongue-lashings) on the way they were bringing up their children; better yet, the way they were failing to bring them up: without discipline, without responsibility, without faith in God or respect for His ministers, without respect for anyone or anything. One of those lost young souls, this priest was sure, had stolen the microphone from the pulpit just recently, before a Mass for the dead got underway, no doubt to support his drug addiction. "Unless," the priest added sarcastically, "the thief is thinking of turning into a radio announcer or a popular comedian, which I doubt very much." None of the parents who attended those prayer meetings had children like the ones this priest was talking about. The parents and children he had in mind were, unfortunately, the very ones who never came to church, so he was really wasting his time and sermons on the innocent. But they tolerated him. He was their priest.

This same padre from Spain was in charge of putting on morality and passion plays during Christmas and Holy Week. Segundo and Moncho took part in them almost every time, playing whichever roles the outspoken priest saw fit to assign them: Judas, Pontius Pilate, one of the good Apostles, Simon of Cyrene (the one who helped Christ carry His cross up to Calvary for no fee), or any one of the villains and cowards who tortured Our Lord.

Segundo and Moncho enjoyed taking part in those sacred dramas, despite the long hours of preparation and the other labors that went into putting on a play properly, competently. Large crowds of worshipers turned out to see them reenacting momentous biblical events up on an improvised stage in the church. They packed the pews and stood up in the aisles for well over two hours, and nobody complained or got out of hand. If anyone passed out from lack of oxygen or from feebleness, he or she was looked to right away without any commotion or hysterics.

That was one harmless way of bringing many people of all

ages and conditions together for a little while twice a year. The actors' only reward for their sweat was a feeling of counting for something, especially when their performance was interrupted by unexpected applause and cheers. "And all for something that feels more like play than like work," Segundo says.

But he hasn't been able to act in one of those sacred dramas in the past three years. Nowadays he's strictly a spectator in the pews. His doctors forbid him to act any more.

Because Magda was wrong when she diagnosed his condition as a cold in the eyes. By the time he got back home that day, his head was still feeling hot, he was still seeing ghosts on either side of him, and he was still feeling dizzy. It took him just as long to get to his building that evening as it had taken him to get to work in the morning.

The following morning, he and Magda went to see Dr. Murillo, who was an ophthalmologist. He subjected Segundo to four hours of intricate tests with all kinds of instruments, and at the end of that period he told Segundo—what Segundo had suspected all along—that he'd had either a stroke or something like it in his sleep. Then Dr. Murillo got on the phone and called up a colleague, Dr. Kawesch, a neurologist-psychiatrist in Mamaroneck. Dr. Kawesch was attached to Albert Einstein Hospital, in the Bronx. When he called Dr. Murillo back, it was to tell him that Einstein would not be able to admit Segundo right away: their cardiology wards were all filled up, no empty beds just then. While waiting for a bed, Segundo was to call him up first thing in the morning and report his symptoms. Under no conditions was he to go back to work.

Next morning, before he called the doctor, Segundo called up Bob and Roy to tell them what the doctor had ordered and why. (This time he had no intention of lying to them.) His bosses told him not to even dream of coming in to work until he was completely cured. They hoped that would be soon, and not just because they were going to have to hobble along with his less-than-perfect assistants. But that was too bad; that was their problem right now, they said. Segundo thanked them. They wished him a quick recovery. He thanked them again, and they all hung up.

On the fifth day after he woke up with the trouble, he was

admitted to Albert Einstein Hospital and spent two weeks there. He had expected the doctors to cut open his chest, like a chicken's (nowadays they used electric saws, he'd heard), but he was wrong on that. There was no need to operate, the doctors said. Instead they put him through a "battery" of routine tests—electrocardiograms, encephalograms, chest X rays, blood samples, urine samples, and the rest—and they gave him pills to slow down his heartbeat and others to bring down his blood pressure; they shot a special dye into his veins to calculate his circulation; they put him on a strict, tasteless diet, and kept him in bed on intravenous glucose, and in a wheelchair most of the time for two weeks.

By the end of that time he felt much better, though not exactly completely cured. His head no longer felt overheated, and the dizziness was gone, but he still had the fuzzy peripheral vision—and always would, the doctors told him: he'd just have to be careful crossing streets from now on. The last piece of advice—actually a strong order—the doctors gave him before sending him home was that on no account must he go back to work. Ever. As far as they were concerned (and this included Dr. Kawesch, who was now his official M.D.), he was a retired worker—for life—a former shipping clerk. If he did not do as they said, he would either have another stroke, from which he was not likely to recover, or he might turn into a vegetable, which he thought was worse than dying. He could take his pick, they said, but don't look at them if he went ahead and disobeyed their orders.

Which of course he didn't. He couldn't.

It took him a few days to recover from the disorientation brought on by two weeks in the hospital, and when he had regained enough control of his senses to conduct a coherent conversation, he called the factory and told Bob and Roy what the doctors at Einstein had told him. His bosses accepted his resignation with deep regrets; they said they didn't see how they were ever going to find a good replacement for him. He thought they would, but he didn't say that. He told them he understood what they meant, and got carried away for a minute: he apologized for the bad turn his health had taken. They told him to forget it; that wasn't his fault. And they wanted to know if there was anything they could do. At the moment, he said, he couldn't think of anything special, but he'd be sure to let them know if anything came up. He'd give it some thought. And they left it at that for the time being.

In the meantime, there was a little practical problem to deal with: the problem of income, how to make up for the loss of his job. For the past three years, Magda had been working at a Bronx high school as a cook's assistant, clean-up lady and table attendant for the students and teachers. Her salary before taxes came to ninety-seven dollars a week. Their son and daughter were holding down part-time jobs, after school and on week-ends, but their combined income, even when added to their mother's, was hardly enough to offset the loss of Segundo's earnings. Maybe Social Security benefits would make up the difference.

Segundo had, of course, all the medical evidence he needed to qualify for those benefits. Probably more than he needed, but that was all to the good. Dr. Kawesch and the cardiologists at Albert Einstein had compiled enough evidence of his condition to convince anyone of his entitlement. "Even this President we're stuck with," he said, half kidding.

Little did he know, though, because it didn't occur to him— and there was no reason it should—that the Social Security doctors and the others who okayed and rejected cases might not see eye to eye with Dr. Kawesch and the Einstein cardiologists.

A few months after he applied for benefits (why the long wait?), he received an official appointment with a doctor who had a contract with the Social Security Administration. This doctor turned out to be a very busy man. Overworked, was what he was. It looked like he was doing the job of two doctors at least, maybe three. Standing room only in his waiting room, and a rapid turnover of patients. Segundo wondered if there wasn't a revolving door or a turnstile installed inside this doctor's consultation room. Whatever he had in there, he was certainly a fast worker; a most efficient M.D., to be sure.

It turned out there was no turnstile inside the examining room, just efficiency. The doctor and his assistant put Segundo through some of the same tests he'd been given at Einstein, only much faster. He asked Segundo some quick questions on his condition, but he seemed bored by the answers. And it was over in ten minutes or less. Outside, the doctor's assistant told Segundo that Social Security would let him know shortly of the doctor's report. He assumed that this examination he'd just been rushed through was not to be taken too seriously; it was just a routine required by law. The real evidence, the decisive evidence, the evidence submitted by Dr. Kawesch and the Einstein specialists, was safe in the files of Social Security downtown. So, as he saw it, he had nothing to worry about, and went home feeling confident: almost, he decided, like a new man.

Two weeks later he hadn't heard anything, so he called the Social Security office, anxious to have his case approved. But the man his call was transferred to told him his case was still pending. He'd just have to be patient, the man said, because there were many other cases like his, many applicants for benefits. Segundo, anxious not to offend, said he understood and apologized for making a pest of himself (he certainly felt like a pest just then). He said he wasn't asking for special treatment, God forbid. But—well, he did have this problem with paying the rent and other expenses, and would appreciate it if—he was beginning to stammer. The official at the other end of the phone, whose breathing was beginning to sound like a symptom of something going wrong with his own heart, said what he'd already said before Segundo interrupted. His case was being processed. Patience was recommended. A couple more weeks. All right.

Three weeks later, nothing. He brought himself to call again with the same question and was given the same answer, this time by a different official: case being considered, patience. He waited another three weeks, the most his anxiety and rising blood pressure would allow, and called again. Same thing. He never spoke to the same official twice. It seemed there were many officials down there, all of them tied up with more important cases than Segundo's, and all of them with the same message for him. By now they must have known who he was before he identified himself, the pest.

But something had to happen, a breakthrough had to be made in his case, and he was right. A month after his last call, he received a docket-numbered form letter, worded in an intimi-

dating prose style, informing him that his application for benefits had been "disallowed." It seemed the doctor who specialized in hasty examinations, and the Board of Final Decisions,
had found nothing seriously wrong with his heart or brain (no
mention was made of his damaged vision), and (it was implied)
he could go back to work tomorrow, or whenever he felt like it.
No benefits.

They must have made a mistake, mixed up his case with
someone else's; that kind of thing was bound to happen in such a
busy organization. So he went down to their office next day
(Moncho drove him down in the Olds, and was late for work; but
so what, he told Segundo). And after a long wait, because he
hadn't made an appointment, the official he spoke to said that
the evidence submitted by their doctor overruled that submitted by Segundo's doctors. However, he was told, he had the
right to appeal, and he was given a form of appeal to be filled
out at home and mailed back at his convenience. He filled it out
that afternoon and mailed it back that night.

After another long wait, he was sent to another overworked
S.S. doctor for another turnstile examination, and three months
later he was found disqualified again. Same document, same
reasons. On principle, he went down again for another explana-
tion, and, as he had expected, was told nothing new. This was
beginning to feel like one of those gloomy endings he and
Magda had seen in dozens of second-rate movies.

That night he called his brother-in-law, the auto mechanic,
who had been retired by something he called "pernicious ane-
mia"; he also had his own heart condition, angina something.
Something Latin. He had qualified for Social Security benefits
without too much trouble. But that was before S.S. was put on a
tight budget by, he told Segundo, "some bastard and his pack
up in Washington. I leave it to you to guess who. And your
particular case came along too late to do you any good."

What his brother-in-law suggested was that Segundo get
more medical proof of his condition, and recommended his own
cardiologist, a specialist who didn't come cheap. It couldn't hurt
to try another, independent opinion.

Segundo no longer had his own medical coverage—could no
longer afford it—but he was covered by Magda's plan, after

deductibles. Those had to come out of his own savings (his and Magda's "retirement money"), which were down to a few hundred dollars.

His brother-in-law's heart doctor gave it to Segundo straight: his heart was "seriously swollen" (poor circulation); so were his ankles (Segundo could see that for himself); he had a heart murmur (he didn't need another doctor to tell him that); his blood pressure was too high (he'd have to control his moods). Nothing new, in other words, except the bill, which was no joke. He hoped he wouldn't get into the expensive habit of consulting more new doctors just to prove to S.S. what S.S. already knew.

His brother-in-law's specialist submitted his findings to S.S., and the slow, expected response Segundo received contained one hopeful note: his case, which had been "terminated," was being reopened. They'd let him know of their decision as soon as they reached one.

The last time he called to ask about the progress of this latest prospect, he was told his case was still pending. This time he almost lost his temper, but he got hold of himself. Giving some anonymous official a piece of his mind wouldn't help his cause one bit. It could only shoot up his blood pressure and swell his heart and ankles some more. So he hung up politely and distracted himself with his dominoes.

Not long after he left Einstein Hospital, he had applied for veterans benefits. He had served two years in the Army; he had spent eighteen months in Korea, in the Quartermaster Corps; and he was still entitled, he assumed, to some help from the VA. After all, he was a disabled veteran now. But he had a thing or two to learn from that administration. When he went down for a hearing, a VA official told him that according to their records he had died back in 1963. He said he hadn't died in 1963, or any other year, as the official could see. "I'm standing right here alive, as you can see," he said. "Do I look dead to you?"

But he was told that his presence there was no proof that he was who he said he was. "We'll need your fingerprints," he was told. He gave them his fingerprints. He was told that they would be sent to the FBI or whoever, and within a few weeks or so the

VA would be in touch with him, let him know whether he was still alive.

Whenever he calls to find out if he's been brought back to life in their records, they tell him his case is being processed, still pending. He calls them less often these days. Like the S.S., they're a very busy outfit, and he doesn't like to make a pest of himself.

Then there was the Department of Social Services, the D.S.S., the people who dispense public welfare. After the necessary red tape and the embarrassing questions (which Segundo suspected might be less necessary than met the eye, and more embarrassing than necessary, perhaps to discourage applicants), he and Magda were found qualified for benefits: $197 a month, a boon. Four months later, though, they received a letter telling them their benefits were being discontinued because their assets exceeded their earnings, meaning that Segundo hadn't declared his jalopy.

That was true, he hadn't: they had him red-handed. He requested a hearing, was granted it, and explained to the caseworker who had the goods on him that he had bought that thing back in 1974, when it was already, quite frankly, fit for a graveyard; but it came in handy sometimes. He rarely drove it, he said, and not just because the cost of gas was so high. He drove it mostly to pick up his daughter at the subway station when she came home from Gimbels at nine o'clock five nights a week. It was cheaper than a taxi, and safer; and it was unsafe for his daughter to be waiting for a bus all by herself at a dark bus stop in the middle of nowhere. The caseworker remarked that, in that case, he could wait with his daughter for the bus. He replied that that was dangerous too, and felt like a coward for saying it, but it was true.

Then he mentioned those Sunday picnics at the state park near Connecticut; he and his wife drove there when the weather permitted. He also told the caseworker about the Wednesday-night group meetings at his parish church; he and his wife no longer dared walk there by themselves. Just the same, he went on, he had lately been thinking of selling that car —"a part-time necessity," he called it—because someone with his heart condition and impaired vision perhaps shouldn't be driving a car.

The caseworker said she couldn't agree more, but that wasn't why they had discontinued his benefits. The long and short of it, she said, was that people on welfare were not supposed to own a car, and he would have to sell his, never mind what condition it was in, if he wanted to remain on the rolls. Nothing he could say in his own defense would change the caseworker's mind. She had nothing to do with it, she said. She was only following departmental regulations. End of hearing.

After three weeks of asking around, Segundo sold the Olds to someone who lived near his building, a dynamic young man who would most likely wreck that jalopy within a month. Segundo sold it to him for eighty dollars, and was sure he had come out ahead. He felt like a thief. But when he presented the "bill of liquidation" to the caseworker, she told him he and Magda were no longer eligible for benefits. He had been classified as a welfare fraud, a very serious charge; people got prosecuted for that. He could apply again in the future, of course; that was his legal right. But right now he shouldn't waste his time and theirs.

Sometime later, he received a document from the D.S.S. informing him that he and his family were eligible for food stamps: ten dollars a month. He and Magda thought it over and decided not to take advantage of the offer. For one thing, it might have been meant as a joke, and they were afraid to risk an embarrassment.

Thinking it over, he decided that maybe the Social Security officials were right: maybe he should go back to work, at least part time. This idleness, he suspected, might be doing him more harm than work would. It so happened that Magda's second cousin, Marina, and her husband, Nemesio, owned a small grocery store out in Queens. They put in six days a week, sometimes seven; they were barely breaking even. It was really not worth all the hours they put in. But they preferred to work as a team, a man-and-wife operation, without bosses, and operating their own business was the only way they could do it. They didn't have any children—they couldn't have any—but they were planning to adopt one or two when they could afford to.

One day Segundo called them up and asked if they could use an assistant for a few hours a week. They knew he was a good worker, but he told them so anyway, and added that, by the way, he wouldn't expect much in the matter of wages. He made it sound as if he were looking for a hobby. He was also putting Marina and Nemesio on the spot. In the first place, they didn't need an assistant; in the second, they couldn't afford one. They had turned down others looking for part-time work in their hole-in-the-wall. But Segundo wasn't exactly another needy stranger: he was practically a member of their own family. They'd known him a long time, and they were perfectly aware of his and Magda's situation. So they gave him the job. No more than fifteen hours a week, though, preferably less: they knew about his heart condition, and they couldn't afford to pay him more than forty dollars. He understood. He appreciated it. They wouldn't regret it. They said they knew that. He knew he was taking unfair advantage of their goodwill, but he was feeling a little desperate (he didn't tell them that).

So he went to work for Marina and Nemesio, commuting by bus to Queens, getting there by eight in the morning (an hour after they opened up for business) and leaving by noon, though sometimes he hung around till one or two, having nothing better to do with himself. His duties were simple: opening up boxes of food and beverages, stocking the shelves, pulling things down from the shelves, taking things down to the cellar, bringing others back up, sweeping, dusting, wiping, scrubbing. Once in a while, when there was a short-lived flurry of business, he helped Marina and Nemesio behind the crowded, narrow counter. Otherwise he stayed out of the way, because there wasn't much room for three in that store. Sometimes he overdid it, though; he worked harder than was necessary, and Marina and Nemesio had to remind him of his heart condition. If something happened to him in their store, they'd feel responsible. He got the message and slowed down a little.

One day he took a train up to Mamaroneck; he'd been having dizzy spells again. Dr. Kawesch told him his blood pressure was way up and his heart was a little larger than last time. In fact, the doctor said, his condition showed an overall deterioration. Had he been pushing himself too much? Had he gone back to work or something? Segundo said he hadn't. He was afraid Dr. Kawesch would wash his hands of him if he told the truth. Dr. Kawesch prescribed the usual and told him the usual: take it easy, take your pills as prescribed, find distractions like TV and dominoes to keep from worrying. Segundo thanked him and went home to relax.

That night, Marina and Nemesio called to say he shouldn't come to the store next day or ever. They told him why. Earlier that day, while he was up in Mamaroneck, a couple of familiar faces had come on a return visit to the store. One of them had a gun, again. And they hadn't come to return the money they had taken with them the last time they paid Marina and Nemesio a visit with that gun. On the contrary, they had come for more of the same, and they wanted it fast, no backtalk.

The one with the gun made Marina and Nemesio lie stomach down on the other side of the counter while his friend emptied the cash register. On the way out, while Marina and Nemesio stared at sawdust, their two visitors helped themselves to a couple of bags of potato chips and fried pork rind. "See you next time," they said. Next time, nothing.

Marina and Nemesio didn't even bother calling the police this time, because the first time it happened, the police took down the details of the holdup and never came around again. Maybe they couldn't be bothered. This was a busy precinct. So Marina and Nemesio decided to liquidate their business and go back where they came from: a small village in Puerto Rico. They might open up another business in the village someday, after they got settled down. Two months after they failed to notify the police, they packed up and left.

Segundo and Magda are pretty sure they would have done the same in their shoes. They haven't given up on the notion of going back home eventually, when their son and daughter get on their own and his Social Security benefits start pouring in. He's patient. "What's a little patience?" he says.

"Thirty-two years," Magda says. And they leave it at that, for now.

One of the Lucky Ones
MARY LEE SETTLE

LIKE THE ELDEST SON IN THE STORY OF THE PRODIGAL, MY cousin Edgar's virtues were not very attractive to me. He always did everything right. I never thought that we had much in common, which is the genteel way of saying that I always disliked his tight face, his mustache, his shoes, his politics. I remember him as tall. When I see him, I'm surprised that he isn't. He was the kind of man who made a vocal point of not cheating on his income tax, although when there was, in his words, a Democrat regime, he squealed like a stuck pig. His form was always filed by January 31.

I felt diminished and somehow ciphered by him. He exuded a kind of judgmental neatness. His life, as he often said, was the Company—no, not the CIA, although I think he might have dreamed of that, as lesser people in his eyes, myself included, dream of flight. The Company was a subsidiary that made some chemical he didn't talk about. I think it was something that hardened steel. It was the only industry in one of those company towns that stretch along the narrow mountain valleys of West Virginia. The parent company—he called it that—is in New York.

When his wife died, I think his loyalty to the Company filled the real gulf she had left. It permeated the whole house, from the buried garbage cans through the two-car garage, with one car, hers, used only on Saturdays to keep it in running order, to the color TV, the den, and the shaved grass. I always saw that loyalty as green, bright green, fertilized loyalty. He never bragged about any of this. I think he never considered that he needed to. It was simply a permeation and a world he had every reason to take for granted.

His den was paneled in wormy pine. The first time I saw it, twenty years ago, he pointed this out.

He said, "Wormy pine. Wormholes cost an arm and a leg, let me tell you!" Then he grinned and his mustache widened. He was thirty-five then and the mustache was already showing faint gray threads. Then he said, apologizing to himself, "It was an excellent investment."

Through the years, the Company spread over one wall, and I could see him at night at his desk, swiveling around to look at it. There was his chemical engineering degree from Carnegie Tech (he had "gone into management" later), a golf trophy from the Company country club on a wall bracket, a certificate that looked like an honorary degree, a framed form letter from President Nixon thanking him for his work in the 1968 election, and photographs of groups at picnics, dinners, conventions, one in front of the pyramids. He was inevitably in the second row, his mustache grayer and grayer.

Two years, ago, when I went back for my grandmother's funeral, nothing had changed or been moved. There were a few more photographs. The silver double frame on his desk was the same one I had always remembered. It contained the imitation Bachrachs, with backlighting, taken when his wife was forty and his daughter was fifteen. Both of them were smiling.

In those days, in the sixties, they seemed to enjoy themselves. They gave cocktail parties with the management men on one side of the living room in winter, or the back garden in summer, the women on the other. In summer their heels sank into the turf. Nobody drank too much or raised their voices. The Company seemed to be present among the trees. Late in the evening the women confessed to using Miracle-Gro.

They were untouched by the tumultuous decade of the sixties, although they freely expressed opinions damning everything in it. They were "for" the Vietnam War. Every Fourth of July, Edgar unfurled an American flag that still had forty-eight stars. His wife was a busy, likable woman. She volunteered. There were long telephone conversations that had to do with personalities and raising money. His daughter, called Mary Lou after her mother, swam the mile in record time. He was proud of them both. They seemed to me to be partly constructed out of Company policy and the L. L. Bean catalogue.

The Company arranged his mortgage and his insurance, health and life. The mortgage was large. He explained every January that this was good business; "taxwise," nobody but a fool paid off a mortgage. It was, he said, an investment. It saved taxes, and the sale value was, in his word, enhanced.

Two years ago, in 1981, the subsidiary closed down. It happened suddenly on a Monday morning a few weeks before I saw him. At first I thought the shock on his face was grief at the death of our grandmother. It wasn't. It was like a person who had been in an earthquake, terra no longer firma. The air had gone out of him and left him a little smaller. For a month there was 100 percent unemployment on the crescent of mock-Colonial houses, but nobody called it that. Then neighbors began to move out and FOR SALE signs went up for the first time since the subsidiary had opened, thirty years before.

His daughter was then thirty-five. She and her husband had bought a house two blocks away, where the lawns were very green and the azaleas a little too gaudy and the streets a series of pleasing arcs that curved up into the hills. None of the trees had been cut down as they are in cheaper housing developments, and everybody repainted every two years, and there seemed to be no mess anywhere. They did it to be near Daddy.

Mary Lou and her husband, Elwood, a dentist, whose main economic joke was "There's always toothaches," had become born-again Christians and members of the 700 Club. They did all the things that went with that. In the evenings she sold soap for Amway. They had the slight, superior, kindly smiles of people who were in on some kind of secret.

They gave up alcohol and cigarettes and swam at the Y, fifteen miles away, in Coalburg. The Company country club, where she had spent her youth, had closed down, and the fairway grass grew meadow tall.

Edgar excused what had happened to him. He said he saw the necessity of amalgamation. "You've got to streamline in today's economy, let me tell you," he said at first. For a while he expected to be transferred, and the only complaint he had was that at fifty-four it would be hard to put down new roots. When he saw the parent company's stock go up and up, he waited to be called back. When he wasn't, he went to the head office in New York and waited to be interviewed by men of forty, who were nice to him and said they would be in touch. He collared whoever he could to take to dinner at the Four Seasons. He stayed at the St. Regis. He said you must never lower your standard of living—that "they" would notice. He took to visiting other chemical companies to let people know he was ready for a change.

He still defended the Company. He said management had tough decisions to make. "Boy, I've had to make plenty myself, let me tell you," he said. After his business trips to New York, he came back talking about "smart young fellows, let me tell you."

After a year he didn't go any more. Gradually he had moved into his den; his living space diminished. I began to feel sorry for him but fought it. It seemed to be an insult to him. Mary Lou didn't. She talked incessantly about poor Daddy. She said she worried about him if he didn't call or come by every day. He said, when he missed a day, that he was too busy. When he went to dinner with them once a week, he glued himself to the television and watched the news as if it were wartime. From time to time he nodded. He explained supply side and the filter-down theory during the commercials. His comments were as rain on a parched and waiting soul.

Mary Lou and Elwood were kindness itself. She said it was her Christian duty after all. She looked through his refrigerator and cupboards to see that he wasn't neglecting himself. She walked around the empty dining room, the living room, the screened-in terrace, like a person inspecting rental property. She found a bottle of bourbon and took it away. The next day she found another one. She told me that Edgar explained to her that it was for medicinal purposes.

But the day in early spring when she found four ounces gone out of it, she cried, and then knelt on the living room floor and prayed aloud to a flock of china ducks across the wall. Beyond her profile I remember almost-naked branches of forsythia outside the picture window. The house was cold. She had asked me to go with her that day, because she said it was getting too much for her. The whole place was as neat as a tomb. All the time she was praying I stood embarrassed. Her voice mingled with the slow beat of two fingers on a typewriter behind the closed door of the den.

He came out finally. He looked dusty. He had not shaved. His clothes, an old pair of jeans and a Miami Dolphin sweatshirt hung on him. I couldn't have guessed he owned such clothes. It was hard to look at him, so I looked away. He sensed it, and I heard him say, "I've got a little problem with my skin." Even his voice was thinner, light, like a man used to whispering.

He tried to make a joke. "Mary Lou, are you out here bobbing to Jesus again?" I could feel his smile on the side of my face. "We're all used to it, aren't we, honey?"

We? There wasn't any we—just the two of them, and me, who didn't want to be there. He touched my arm. "I sure am glad to see you, Coz," he said, "damn, it's been too long."

He went straight to the abandoned sofa and said, "Mary Lou, honey, I've got to talk to you and I want Coz here to hear this. Now, don't get all upset." She sat rigid, not looking at either of us. Obviously, "don't get all upset" had been the harbinger of bad news all her life. He told her the house was too big for him, that he had put it on the market. They sat in the living room talking as if they didn't know each other very well. He said he was sure the house would bring a hundred "thou." He told me he had paid only forty "thou." "I've got my eye on a condo, maybe in Florida. After all . . . ," he said.

Mary Lou began to count assets. "Let's see . . . with your profit . . . your savings . . . , let's see. . . ."

Then it came out as if he wanted to get rid of it. "I've run through that."

She just stared at him. She looked like one of those comic book cartoon characters with button eyes.

Edgar leaned back and stuck his feet way out over the carpet. He was wearing sneakers without socks. His whole body seemed to deflate with relief. He had lost the tension that comes with giving a damn. "I was investing in my future," he said, and he laughed.

There was not a sound.

Then he said, wanting to get it all over, "I cashed in my life insurance." Silence. "Well, honey, this is it." He waved at the ducks and the picture window.

"Your *life* insurance," she finally spoke. The word "life" hit high C. "Papa," a little lower but not much, "why didn't you consult *us?*" High again. "You've abdicated all responsibility!" Then she began to cry.

Six months ago the house was sold to a plumber from Coalburg, which has sent out tentacles of suburbs almost to the abandoned company town. Edgar didn't make much. Enough, he says, glaring at Mary Lou, to keep him in cigarettes and liquor.

There wasn't enough of what he now calls money and Mary Lou's husband, Elwood, still calls equity to buy a condo or anything else. He lives with them. Mary Lou tells us all, not caring if he hears her, that it's their Christian duty and that they're glad to have him. You can hear her underline glad.

She tells me it hasn't been easy. She says she told him that the guest room was his, that she wanted him to be entirely at home. But she says he just wasn't considerate. He wanted to hang all that old junk from his den on the wall when she had just redecorated and she simply couldn't let him do that. She says he keeps it in a box under his bed. He complains if young Mary Lou talks too long on the phone. He says he's expecting a call. "I had to put my foot down," Mary Lou says. "He ran up an exorbitant telephone bill, all those calls to New York. Nobody calls back."

Edgar says that he is convinced that things are turning around.

The suburb has changed. There are pickup trucks in the driveways, and the grass looks like it has burst its prison. Elwood has grown a mustache, too, and has begun to drink beer again. He watches the football games on Sunday. He has always tried to have a lot in common with his patients. When you go there, Mary Lou sends little Mary Lou to get "Gramps."

Little Mary Lou is fourteen, nearly six feet tall, and is on the Christian Brotherhood swimming team. They show Gramps off. He is fifty-six. Mary Lou has made some rules. She says she had to. He can smoke only in his room. No liquor. Edgar's breath smells strongly of peppermint. She said he sent out a whole file of résumés, without consulting her. He stays at home and waits.

Mary Lou says she can't get him out of the house. "He won't take a bit of exercise," she says, looking at him.

Elwood says he has to read the paper first, before he goes to work, and Mary Lou says that makes Gramps sulk. "He's spoiled rotten," she says, "but I keep telling him he's luckier than most. What if he had no place to go?"

It is easy to convince the convinced, and to sympathize with the sympathetic. What I have tried to do in this story is to draw attention to another kind of economic neglect. Although empathy with this man is harder, he is as much—though more subtly —a victim of the inhuman decisions of the Reaganite economic atmosphere as any other man who has lost his life support and has nothing left to sustain him. It is fiction because I wanted to reflect in it, from fragments of observation, the lives of a whole body of "good Americans" at management level who are doubly forgotten: forgotten not only by the corporations who have betrayed them, but by the whole system of values they have taken for granted and helped to sustain.

The Empty House

EARL SHORRIS

ON JULY 13, 1980, THE REPUBLICAN NATIONAL CONVENTION opened in Detroit. The Reagan campaign had chosen the most symbolic structure in the city for its headquarters, the new Detroit Plaza Hotel, the towering centerpiece of the downtown redevelopment effort that had been named The Renaissance. From his suite on the twenty-sixth floor, Ronald Reagan directed his campaign, chose his running mate, sold supply-side economics to the nation, and promised in confidential tones to visitor after visitor that he would dismantle the New Deal to save America. He would cut taxes, reduce spending on social programs, strengthen defense, end deficits, stop inflation, get America off the dole and back to work.

Since then, the hotel complex in which Mr. Reagan stayed has failed; the owners could not pay the mortgage; the Aetna Life Insurance Company foreclosed on The Renaissance. It will have to be refinanced. Where once, in July, the press and public clambered up the ramps over the moatlike entrance to the hotel and milled like delighted sheep in the flowered halls and corridors, it is now cold and empty and gray, and a winter wind off the river chills the few people on the way to their bargain-rate rooms.

The failure of The Renaissance may seem a curiosity, the stuff of which propaganda is made, but there are repetitions; the default may be exemplar: Reaganomics has come to Detroit like a plague.

During the Convention a liberal group offered free bus tours of the inner city to delegates, alternates, and the press. Few chose to go. It was hot: the air felt more like Houston than the Canadian border; business could best be carried on in air-conditioned rooms. Had the delegates or the press taken the tour,

they would not have been impressed. Detroit had not repaired
the damage of the riots of the sixties; there was a sort of Forty-
second Street of hustlers and whores and pornography in the
heart of the city, a long, ugly street that eventually turns into a
suburban boulevard; the housing stock was old and uncared for;
poor black children played barefoot in the summer streets. The
South Bronx is more startling, Watts is more depressing, Chicago's ghetto is more sprawling.

More than a few of Mr. Reagan's supporters made jokes about
the tour, which they considered symptomatic of the wrong-
headedness of liberalism; they were against pity and for prosperity, something like two cars in every garage, in honor of the
host city.

Cabdrivers, bellhops and waiters understand national politics
through examining the purse strings of conventioneers. They
are gladdened by the arrival of Democrats and the departure of
Republicans. Something about the character of the two groups
is revealed at conventions, according to those who serve them:
Democrats are givers, Republicans are takers. The cabdrivers
and the bellhops and the waiters could have gone on holiday
while the Republicans took buses, carried their own luggage,
and left ten-cent tips. The economic disappointment of the
convention was a harbinger.

From the windows of the defaulted tower of The Renaissance, one can see that Hudson's Department Store has closed
and the notion of a brilliant and bustling mall for downtown
Detroit has been abandoned. The wreckage of the riots has still
not been repaired. There is something new, however. In the
Cass Corridor, Detroit's one-story midwestern Bowery, there is
a long line of people standing out in the cold. It is sixteen
degrees. The people are stamping their feet, pulling their hands
into their sleeves, hiding their faces in hoods and scarves and
old shirts. A few are dressed in winter clothes that might have
been used by explorers of the Arctic, most are trussed into
layers of all they own, figures so stuffed they have difficulty
withdrawing their hands from the cold into the protection of
their clothing. The line extends from the doorway of a church
down the block to the corner and around the corner onto Cass
Street. At the end of the line is a soup kitchen. Six days a week

two meals are served by the church to those who might otherwise starve in the city that is home to General Motors and Ford, the largest and second-largest industrial organizations in the history of the world.

Food is also distributed at a dozen other churches in Detroit and at the Salvation Army. General Motors and the United Auto Workers have just completed a drive to collect food and money for the poor—they say there will be enough for four million meals. The people of West Germany send food to Detroit, saying they have not forgotten the food that came from America when Germans were starving after the war.

Hunger in Detroit is real; no one in that city denies it any more. In the years since the flags were flying along the promenade between Reagan headquarters and the convention hall, the infant mortality rate has risen steadily in the state of Michigan, twenty-two hundred schools have dropped out of the school lunch program, the city of Pontiac has dropped out of the school breakfast program. Thirty-eight percent of the people in southeastern Michigan receive some kind of state or federal aid. Two thirds of the pregnant women, infants, and preschool-aged children eligible for supplementary food and medical care under the WIC (women-infants-children) program have been put on the waiting list. The cutbacks in social programs have brought the problem of hunger back to Detroit. George Covintree, Jr., director of the Southeastern Michigan Food Coalition, who offers the statistics, says the problem has reached "crisis proportions."

Everyone knows what happened in Detroit, but some are afraid to talk about it. Under the new administration in Washington there are purges, they say, subtle kinds of punishment. They point to a new thrust in government, a new ambiance. One of the people, who fears identification, said, "Programs are so restrictive that the newly unemployed can't get in. The whole situation has exacerbated tensions between poor and working-class people. Newly laid-off people say, 'If I was black and lived in Detroit, I could get plenty.' They're also surprised that welfare is so little. Instead of making people understand how poor welfare support is in this country, the unemployment and the cutbacks in social programs have turned people against each other."

At the close of his acceptance speech, in Joe Louis Arena, the presidential nominee of the Republican Party said, "There's something I know I shouldn't do. It's not part of my speech. But I want to go ahead and do it anyway. Can we begin our crusade joining together in a moment of silent prayer?" He bowed his head for twenty seconds. Then he raised his beaming, triumphant, ancient face to the crowd, to the world, and he proclaimed, "God bless America!"

A mile and a half west and five miles north of the defaulted tower of The Renaissance, another mortgage company has foreclosed on another structure. In two days the small brick-and-shingle house of one gable will be sold at auction. After the sale, no one will move into the house. In a week or two, by accident or malice or design, there will be a fire. Insurance money will be collected. The burned-out shell of the house will stand for a few months, until the city of Detroit sends a bulldozer to knock it down. Then the grass will grow over the rubble in another empty lot on the west side of Detroit.

Something has been taken from this house and from the family inside it. The taking of this thing is a kind of murder, as if the breath or blood had been drained slowly, over the years, over the generations. The last of the draining is underway now, and it is no longer so subtle that the family does not feel pain. Even so, one must do more than merely look and listen to detect the murder. The signs are clear, but one must scrutinize the situation, concentrating on Barbara Piney's house until it becomes a passable mirror.

Concentration will be difficult, for poverty is not interesting, either to the poor or to the rich. It is the curse of the decent poor to be so utterly uninteresting that immoral people can hide them and moral people cannot find them. A certain lurid excitement attends the Piney family, however, for the very subtlety that makes their murders difficult to detect teases our sense of the unsuspected danger that may lie in wait for any of us.

The facts of the family are unexceptional. Aunt Hazel tells the ancient history: Her father had a farm in Mount Olive, Mississippi. It was a big place on good land; the family was well off. He lost the farm in the last Depression, and he had to go North to look for work. He settled into a laborer's life in Detroit. The good times were gone forever. Hazel, her brother Earl, and her sister, Barbara's mother, grew up on the west side.

Aunt Hazel married a man who works at the Ford plant; a good man, she says, with whom she's had a good life. Now, in late middle age, she's big, a woman of girth, with rolls of prosperity all around. Her face is wide and flat; she smoothes and pales it with powder. The southern sweetness remains in her voice even though she has lived most of her life between the freeways and factories of Detroit.

Aunt Hazel and her husband live in one of the two flats in a building they own in an aging development on the other side of the freeway. They have no children. Barbara is almost her child; Barbara's children are almost her grandchildren. Sweet, generous Aunt Hazel, who could hold a family together by her will alone, bustles through Barbara's house. She cooks and cleans and keeps the children occupied whenever she comes to visit. She drives to the store, buys candy, puts pennies in piggy banks. She is a lesson in sweetness and busyness and generosity and the inability of anyone anywhere in the world to get a free lunch. The will of Aunt Hazel weighs heavily in the house: she can spin Barbara around with a glance.

Barbara Piney was still a girl when her parents separated. Her mother had a rheumatic heart; she couldn't work. There was no money. Barbara describes herself ruefully as the second generation on Aid. "I spent a lot of time taking care of my mother," she said. "That's part of the reason why I dropped out of school. My mother was afraid to be alone. She couldn't walk across the room because of that rheumatic heart. She passed away at thirty-seven.

"ADC is good, if you can't do better. But I would like to see my daughter be an achiever. Aid is not something I wanted to do for myself, but my situation hasn't let me get out of it. I've tried with little jobs here and there, but none of the jobs I've had paid hospitalization or whatever. I couldn't do it. The system is set up to keep you behind, to keep you on Aid. All the mothers I know on ADC are striving to get off. People want to be independent."

There is time on AFDC, more as the last child goes to school, time for remembrance and regret. When it is not hard time, it is heavy time. The sense of failure and dependence has been transmogrified by the Reagan administration. "I feel like a diseased person," Barbara said, "like an insect. There are a lot of people that misuse the system, even the rich, but when we're attacked, it stereotypes the average poor person. It hurts a lot because it's not true. We don't like being where we are."

In the heavy time—at night or in the winter when the children are all in school and the house is quiet and there is nowhere to go and nothing to do—she has begun to think:

> I could have done so much better, if I had known, if I had the right type of guidance. I wouldn't have dropped out of school. I probably wouldn't have had my first child. Those two factors alone would have made a big difference.
>
> A person's environment makes a world of difference. It does a lot for their self-esteem. Even as a kid, I had a low esteem. I had many complexes. There were so many things I felt I didn't like about myself. There were so many things I had to do to make people like me. I see a lot of those things in my son, Terry, and I try to make him feel better about himself. My mother and father were good people, but they just weren't aware of my needs. And if they had been, they wouldn't have known what to do.
>
> I had a complex about my nose and I had a burn on my arm and I didn't like my legs. They called me Hook; you know how cruel children can be. There were so many things I didn't like: my hair was always nappy, my clothes were always raggedy. I didn't get real good care.
>
> I didn't realize how much I didn't like myself until about three years ago, when I had my revelation about how my life worked out this way. At about thirty or thirty-one it happens to everyone. I started asking myself what caused me not to be successful. I started writing down what I did. For example, when I did get a job, I would go home after work. I didn't socialize. I didn't go to the parties. They would do things I

didn't do, smoke weed and all. The girls I worked with were the same; we didn't mingle. I wasn't an outgoing type of a person. I always found myself misunderstood. I might even have scared off men because I was so nice. A lady looks for security where a man looks for pleasure.

Her eyes glisten, she smokes a cigarette, inhaling fitfully, nervously; there is no pleasure in smoking for her. She lifts her eyebrows into a weeping arch, as if to say that the conclusions one draws about her are wrong. Yes, she has three children and she has never had a husband; yes, the children carry her name; still, it doesn't have to mean what people think—the pleasure went to the men, exclusively to the men. She was too good, too nice. This is the kernel of her life. She sits quietly for a long time, looking out into the cold, misting rain, waiting, making sure that the words signify.

Barbara lives in the basement of the house, in the room without a door, in the room with the gas furnace and the old, dead refrigerator and the battered washing machine. She lives beneath the exposed heating ducts and electrical wires. Her bed is a mattress; the headboard is the cement-block wall of the basement. She has hung what might once have been bedspreads on some portions of the walls. At night, lying in her bed, she looks at an old, institutional-green freezer that sits precariously on the uneven basement floor. She hears the rumble of the compressor. At night, when she seeks to dream in the hours before sleep, she looks up at the naked underside of a floor. It is a room without a closet or a window, the room with no door. The dressing table is the chipped, mustard-yellow top of a washing machine. The washstand is a gray laundry sink. The toilet is two floors up.

The odor insinuated into natural gas so that it will not go unnoticed is a winter guest in the room where Barbara lives, and in all the other rooms of her house. The odor has been there so long that no one notices it.

"I turned my bedroom into a TV room for the children," Barbara said. In that dark room, a couch and a chair slump on the bare floor. The shapes of the couch and the chair are vague, hidden by dark-colored blankets or pieces of yard goods that have been draped over the old rounds of arms and backs. Something is wrong with the tilt of the furniture; it is leaning under its camouflage, telling of escaped cotton, springs untied, wood cracked, unglued.

One suspects a different cause for the TV room. Perhaps the furniture was once in the living room, which is now empty but for a low, rectangular chest. Perhaps the furniture doesn't live there any more because it was too old, too poor, because Barbara couldn't bear its legs or its raggedy clothes. The drain of the world of making do means living with less and less, with the discovery that ingenuity wanes and that one chair cannot occupy two spaces.

A long time ago—she cannot remember when—her dreams were affected: She lies in bed at night thinking of the future, but it is always *the future*, and it is called *school* or *independence* or a *better world*. The future has no content, she cannot touch the future, she has never seen it. The future is a change of luck, the big break, esteem. "I don't really see things in those dreams," she said; "I guess my dreams are abstract." She nods once, wearily, as if to say that in such dreams there is no place to rest her head.

"All I have is time."

She gardens, except in winter; she washes; she cooks; she cleans; hers is the cleanest house, the most immaculate house. There are three children living here in the dreary, damp, muddy winter of 1983 in Detroit, and the floors of the house are spotless. There is no dust in the house, there is not a mark on the walls, the children's rooms are perfectly neat, in perfect order. The red plastic milk crates that serve as chests and cupboards and occasional tables throughout the house are neatly stacked. One can see into them, into the tidiness, into the emptiness of almost all the chests and cupboards made of red plastic milk crates.

The floors are warm, except for the cement floor in Barbara's room. She walks barefoot through her house, a woman not five feet tall, with straightened hair, skin the color of tobacco stain, Semitic features: a desert nose, a mouth that becomes a crescent when she smiles, heavy eyelids over enormous eyes. She wears jeans and a dark brown cardigan sweater, her winter outfit along with the tennis shoes she keeps near the back door.

Some tension occupies Barbara. Her words often come in bursts. Her eyebrows arch too high, her mouth becomes too narrow, she smokes too hard when the intensely troubled parts of her life come forward, as if those parts could ever recede very much now that the mortgage company has foreclosed and her dreams have become abstract. It is after her revelation, but she sits uncertainly, as if in opposition to the pull of gravity on her heavy hips, squirming when she speaks of men or marriage, of her love for her first child and her wish that there had been free abortions then.

It was not so long ago—nineteen sixty-seven—that Barbara was filled with dreams and singing. She keeps the remains of that time in a thin stack in one of the red plastic milk crates. There are a few folded, crumbling pieces of paper, three photographs, two postcards, a seven-inch 45-rpm record. The group was called The Devotions; Barbara Piney sang lead. It was Motown time. The hits were coming out of the Detroit recording studios like Cadillacs rolling off the line. Detroit was booming, money seemed to be there just for the taking; expectations ran so high a riot was brewing. The record by The Devotions made some of the charts. "Same Old Sweet Lovin' " was the play side, backed by "Devil's Gotten into My Baby." In the grand tradition, the group went on tour: three girls recently dropped out of high school, one of the girls pregnant, a manager/agent/A&R man, and a couple of musicians, vacuum-packed into a worn-out station wagon. They went south from Motown, playing one-nighters in small towns as well as in D.C., Little Rock, New Orleans, Jackson, Mississippi, and on up through St. Louis on the way home.

They headed south in the first week of 1967 and stayed on the road for three months. The tour was a triumph—they broke even, and they never missed a meal or had to sleep in the car. That was the only record, the only tour.

Barbara handles her souvenirs carefully. In one of the photographs she is very pregnant. "I didn't mind that I was pregnant," she said, "but everyone else did. Maybe they thought I wasn't dependable or something. I think that's why they didn't release the other records." She makes no comment, not even a shrug, and moves on to the next photograph: the composers, two young men dressed in mustaches and dark glasses. The last photograph shows The Devotions in what is either a half-finished or very run-down recording studio: some of the acoustic tiles seem to be missing from the wall behind the group. She says that the photograph wasn't made during the actual recording session; they reassembled several weeks later to pose for it. All the photographs are gray; they have the failure of dimension that comes of passing light through a fixed-focus lens.

She looks at her notices, opening them one by one, careful with the slick paper, which has gone dark at the folds as if the clay had returned to its true color. The notices are nothing more than listings. All but one are without comment, and it says, "R/B ditty, good for dancing." There was one mention of the group in a newspaper. The page of newsprint was tinted yellow or orange, a color that has turned or faded to peach over the fifteen fallow years. The mention was somewhere in the middle. She turns the crumbling page over and over, but she cannot find the words about the group.

The dozen souvenirs function for her as intended. "We did an advertisement," she says about the picture postcard from Little Rock. "We were on the play list in Jackson. We had three days in D.C." The group had gone south toward home, to towns like the towns where the family farms had been, to play to crowds where the people looked and talked down home. They had been awaited and applauded. After three months everything stopped. There was no money from the record, there was nothing left from the tour. One of the girls joined another group; Barbara's first child was born. "I was the lead singer," Barbara said, "I *was* the group." It is her moment of animation; her stage presence emerges to recall the dream; the tenth-grader all dressed up and on tour speaks: "And I saw fame and fortune."

After the child, after the disintegration of the group, she moved in with her aunt, who cared for her child, then for her children while Barbara worked. She got a general education diploma, took a course at a community college. In 1974 she was working as a spot welder at a Chrysler plant in Detroit. The money was good, the work was steady. The oil shortages had shaken the auto companies, but everyone was certain that the bedrock of American industry was solid—Chrysler was not General Motors, but it was still one of the biggest manufacturing organizations in America. Barbara homesteaded the little house two blocks from the freeway on the west side.

When she moved in, the paint was new, the carpeting was new, everything was clean and in perfect repair. Even the wiring and plumbing were new. She paid $15,500 for the house, $165 a month to the mortgage company to start, with the payments to rise slowly over thirty years. It cost her $400 to move in. She had some furniture, draperies in a layaway plan that could be hemmed to fit the windows in the new house, appliances, television. It was a complete household. She was elated. That was in January. She had been at Chrysler for almost a year. Soon afterward she was laid off for the first time. It was a week off and a week on, two weeks off and a week on. She had to pay a baby-sitter; she couldn't be sure of when she would work, what she would earn. Finally, she had to leave the job and seek Aid. It was the end of what she calls independence. She had fallen into the pattern; she was the second generation on AFDC.

"People talk about a depression," she said, "but I feel like I've always been in a depression. I've had to sacrifice. It's hard now, but it's always been hard. I'm used to having to struggle; it's not a big thing for me. But as long as I've been on ADC I've been in a depression."

The payments for the house have risen to $198 a month. Some utility bills are paid direct; some she must pay. Her food stamps have been cut. School lunches aren't the same. Bus transportation for her daughter is no longer free. She feels the squeeze. "My older boy has only one pair of pants. He wears them every day. For my baby I got clothes from a friend. When you're on Aid you can't buy seven pairs of pants so they don't wear out. You can't buy cheap pants, because they bust out of them and they don't stand up to many washings."

She's describing her life at the end of a binge, a spending spree unlike anything else she can remember in the nine years that she has been on AFDC. It began when the sewer backed up in her house: "I went to the caseworker and said that I needed plumbing, electrical work, and plastering done. They gave me a book of contractors to call. But those people won't come out, because they know ADC will only take the lowest bid. Well, then my sewer backed up, so I had to get the work done. But the Aid wouldn't pay, because I didn't get the three estimates while the sewer was backing up into the house. So I fell behind when I paid a hundred and eighty dollars to the plumber. That was in September.

"Then I couldn't make the October payment. When I could pay October, it was November and they wanted two months or nothing. They sent me warning letters and all, but they wouldn't accept my payment. And once I got behind on my house note, ADC wouldn't pick up the electric or water bills. So I got a shutoff notice and I had to pay them. Then I got further behind. All through it I was saving. But I took three hundred dollars to buy my kids coats and shoes to go to school. That was at Christmas. Now I have five hundred dollars and I owe twelve hundred dollars.

"When I got the foreclosure notice I didn't cry. Crying doesn't help my situation any. But I never stop thinking about it. As far as tears, I'm cried out. But I think about it. I think about it every hour.

"I love this house. I'm not so crazy about the neighborhood, but I love the house. There are break-ins around here, but my neighbors and I pull together. The kids have conflicts with other kids, but I get along. We have a lot of vacant lots around here. Everybody doesn't try to maintain their property. Maybe because of health reasons. The majority of people in the neighborhood are older people. Maybe they don't have the energy I have."

The neighborhood has no energy. The houses crouch on the flat land, row after row, relieved only by the empty places where the fires are burned out and the rubble is bulldozed. There are few cars in the streets. There are no people walking, nothing moves except the dogs prowling inside the chain-link fences, big dogs, murmuring, barking at anything that moves, at any sudden odor on the wind. The breeds of the dogs can no longer be ascertained; they are just big and surly, walking the muddy perimeters of the tiny yards behind the narrow houses, dogs as mean and depressing as the peeling paint of the houses, dogs as alienating as the chain-link fences that contain them. The warnings barked by the dogs echo in the empty streets, down the rutted grass alleys between the fences.

Barbara has never been to the hamburger joint at the end of the next block, not even to buy a cup of coffee, not in nine years. People on Aid do not go to restaurants or hamburger joints, not ever, not even for a cup of coffee. Nor do people on Aid leave the neighborhood, because bus fare is expensive.

"I joined the Unity Light of Truth Church about five years ago," Barbara said. "A friend had told me about it. I went to one of the services and I liked the message, so I joined. All kinds of people belong, white and black. It serves the community. The church I belong to is in the Cass Corridor. The church gives away food and has clothing drives and all. If I was to go every Sunday, I'd have to take a couple of buses. For the kids and me, that's four dollars, and I just don't have the money. Even if I can get a ride back, I don't have the money to get there. So we don't go. I'm so isolated from the city by the distance, I can't even really take care of business.

"All day I do what I can, but most things take money. I don't have a lot of friends. I've never been a party person. I don't go out that much, I don't have the money. After I do the daily drill with the kids, I don't have the energy to do much more."

Nothing political happens in Barbara Piney's life. She liked John F. Kennedy, she likes everything she has heard about Franklin Delano Roosevelt. She sort of liked Jimmy Carter. "Ronald Reagan's major aim isn't geared for poor people," she said. She thinks he's a racist; she's sure of that. The only thing remotely political she ever did was to attend a meeting of the Black Madonna Lodge of the Shriners. "I'm not a political person," she said. "I would love to be, but I've never had the time. It's not convenient. In a way I believe a little toward the socialist way. I might be a communist. It would be a much better world, a more peaceful world. It would be more equal; there would be less crime. No one would be poor or in need of Aid. Everyone would have a job. The rich wouldn't have it all, like they do now."

With difficulty she recalls where she heard of this "ism" that holds so much promise for peace and equality. It was in a political science course—the only one she ever attended—during her weeks at Wayne County Community College.

The house and the things of the household, limited by the insidious diminishing of a budget lower than enough, defines Barbara Piney's life. The highlights are the children: La Keisha is the dream child, fifteen years old, the winner of a trophy for dancing, a compact, graceful child, smooth of feature, smooth of movement, a liquid child, still in the age of laughter, soon to enter the age of sidelong glances and fretting.

"I always tell all of them: don't be as good as I am. Be better. Always strive to be better than me. I don't tell her what she should be. I always try to install work. You must work. Don't be like me or you'll suffer like me. La Keisha is the most responsible. I'm on Aid, my momma was on Aid, but Keisha's going to be independent. I want her to be the one to get off Aid.

"And look at Andre. Each year is better with him, even his grades. His whole personality is improving. He was my hardest kid. He had a low esteem, like I did. But I worked with him. I spent time with him to help his esteem.

"They're all more work-oriented than I was when I was coming up. I take more time with them than was given to me when I was a kid. It takes energy. That was something my mother didn't have. And my father didn't have patience."

Andre is eleven years old. He would like to be a dentist. His practice is small now, confined to himself and his younger brother. He pulls teeth, but only after they're loose. To reduce pain, he said, "I use stuff in a tube, like Superglue." He is the most winning of the children, chubby, quick, with the same tension under laughter that defines his mother. There is an almost angelic look about him, as if he has survived some suffering by rising above it into a state of nervous beatitude. He is close to his mother, proud that she sang with The Devotions. He knows the souvenirs; his lips form the names of the towns when she tells of the tour. Andre wears his one pair of trousers.

The baby, Major, is only six years old. Barbara says he was the easiest, as Andre was the most difficult. Major is expert in the role of youngest child. He is Aunt Hazel's favorite, which gets him rides to the store to buy wax candy filled with sweet juice, chewing gum, and change to put in his penny bank. Major is light-skinned, almost pale. He seems delicate compared to everyone else in the family, lacking vigor. He squirms. Perhaps it is his age or merely the youngest child doing business.

In the middle of Sunday morning, Barbara Piney stands barefoot in the kitchen, stirring chicken dressing in a pot, while the chicken bakes and the potato salad chills. The children wake up late. They stay upstairs until Sunday dinner is ready. A meal is skipped, the budget is stretched. Barbara has learned to survive on four hundred dollars a month, all that is left in food stamps and Aid after paying for her mortgage and utilities. It could be divided out to a little more than a dollar per meal per person if no one in the family ever needed clothing or soap or toothpaste or bus fare, if Barbara didn't smoke and Major didn't have a craving for wax candy filled with sweet water and Andre didn't need some sort of local anesthetic to aid his dentistry, if the gas bill and the phone bill didn't have to be paid, if La Keisha wasn't going to be a woman tomorrow and the ceiling didn't need painting and it didn't cost twenty-five dollars to get someone to cut down the dead tree in the backyard. Even though the family has learned to use toilet paper instead of Kleenex, and paper towels instead of paper napkins, it still costs money to buy toilet paper and paper towels. It takes a lot of soap to make a house so tidy and clothes so clean.

Barbara doesn't have a dollar a meal for each of them; she has the forty-six cents per meal now considered adequate in the Food Stamps Program.

"I buy canned goods. I cut plenty of coupons. And I always buy the cheapest. I may find a brown spot on the green beans, but I want them to last through the month. I buy the no-name brands. As far as personal things, I wait for the sales. I think I'm a good cook; the kids eat everything. The meat I feed them most is hamburger and chicken, because I can do so many different things with them.

"I make meat loaf, spaghetti—spaghetti is their favorite—Beefaroni, barbecued chicken, fried chicken, hot dogs, hamburgers. We do a lot of baking, me and Keisha. We bake all of the sweets ourselves. It's cheaper to buy the flour and the butter than the sweets that are in the stores.

"From month to month when I get my little check, it's gone. I would like to save, but I don't have anything to save. The kids don't go hungry. If I do run short, my aunt helps me; she picks up my slack."

In the backyard, strips of ground have been cleared of grass for a garden. Barbara plants vegetables there: string beans, wax beans, peppers, squash, tomatoes, beets, collards, mustard, turnips, strawberries, and onions. She had the tree chopped down so there would be more sun for the vegetables. When the harvest is good, she freezes the surplus of summer for use in winter. She is proud that at the end of winter there are still plastic bags full of green beans in the freezer, although she admits sheepishly that Aunt Hazel adds the surplus of her garden to Barbara's freezer.

The fence is down on one side of the yard; someone or something has trampled the green onions—the tops lie broken in the mud. The dogs across the rutted alley snarl, pacing along the inside of the steel fence. The whole backyard of Barbara Piney's house is no more than six or eight hundred square feet of grass and weeds edged in strips of mud, slashed by a mud path that leads to the garbage cans in the alley.

The house, her home, looms enormous in Barbara's life. "The house is the only thing of material value that I have," she said. "It gives me a sense of security. Having it makes me feel as if I can achieve. Without it, I'd feel a lot worse emotionally. If I should lose the house, I know it's time to move on to something better. It would only make me work harder. But I just don't believe I'm gonna lose the house. I just have the feeling that something is going to manifest itself. I pray every day, all day, and it didn't just start. I don't consider myself a devoutly religious person. I just believe in God."

In two days the tidiest house in West Detroit will be sold at auction, unless Barbara's case worker wants to stop it or the Legal Services Office in Michigan can make an arrangement through the courts permitting her to keep the house while continuing her payments at a higher rate, perhaps forty dollars a month more. She can only imagine what will happen when she has forty dollars less each month.

Nothing but a chest and green draperies are left in the living room of the Piney house. The rug of nine years ago has been patched with another rug from another homestead house of the same time; the seams glare at Barbara; she cannot see the floor without noting the seams. In the dining area are a table of metal and plastic, three torn metal-and-plastic chairs, a dark wood hutch and a sideboard, and on the wall a repaired painting of the sort that decorate motel rooms. The painting was given to Barbara, because the plastic frame, which is of a piece with the painting, was badly torn. She repaired the mock wood with a piece of electric cord, and she did it well, as she patched and painted the ceiling well in the dining room and in the bedrooms.

What she cannot do with the house is fill it with herself and her family. Nor can she mark the house with things that are the signs of who they are. The one sign that is uniquely hers was written in a small patch of cement at the base of the front steps: God Bless You. She calls it her mark. It is her only mark. The tidy house is empty of the made or purchased choices of life. What little adorns it has been cast off by acquaintances and strangers, then accepted, found, accommodated, like the weather or the hour, no more made, no more owned. As the house is empty, so is the street empty. Loneliness has drained all odors but the odor of gas, all flavor, all light from the house, from the street, the neighborhood, the near west side.

Poverty has disconnected the family from itself and the world around it. The murder is revealed as the draining of culture by means of generations of confinement inside a diminishing space. That is the horror. These are people formed by television and now too bored by television to watch it. No newspapers, no magazines come into this house. The only books were gifts of the Unity Light of Truth Church of Unity Village, Missouri. The music is manufactured; it relates to the human experience in the manner of detergents, cheese spreads, and false fingernails.

The Piney house is empty, small; the walls are coming together, the ceiling is drawn down toward the floor. The windows of the house are tightly packed with paper to keep them from rattling when the factory down the block runs its big machines late at night. Life in the house is confounded by space: the distance between the Piney family and the rest of the world cannot be traversed, poverty is a moat around them, but inside the moat the family is packed so tightly it cannot breathe.

In the flat accents of the Midwest one can hear the dying of the language that was their birthright. They are without the things of which metaphors are made. There are no woods or creeks in west Detroit; there is no local history. The Pineys are made to speak the words of the blue light of television and supermarket aisles, the words that are not words, the intolerable inflation of language that displaces the real things on which imagination must be founded.

The mailman drops the check into the box and goes on to the next house; the money is spent in the supermarket; no word need be spoken.

In two days the sheriff will auction the Piney house. Then everyone will leave. The silence of the street will be greater than ever. The blight that has stripped the trees of their bark and left the wood to bleach like bones in a desert will spread upward into the last living branches, the paint will separate from the wood of the houses and burst and fester like sores, the dogs will maintain the fearsome gulfs between the remaining people of the neighborhood by fixing them with snarls and yellow eyes; then nothing will happen, nothing, not a thing.

Barbara will continue to look for the promise of history in some *ism* she cannot quite recall. She will ponder metaphysics as explained by the books from Unity Village, Missouri. In a world without concrete dreams, any abstraction will do.

Roosters and Saints

RON ARIAS

LAST WEEK I WAS PULLED HOME BY A ROOSTER, A SCRAWNY, whitish creature three months old and yellowing around the edges. He lived under a ventilated milk-carton crate, which itself had been squeezed and tucked into a corner crowded with shoes of all sizes, and piled-on clothes hung from nails in the walls. This rooster, when freed and allowed to roam the apartment three or four times a day, made the same movements all chickens do: jerky tilts of the head, eyeballing the world for food, now and then lifting a graceful, splayed foot an inch or two into the air, motionless, then moving on, ever searching, ever dumb. At the same time, a white pigeon flew from the top of the refrigerator, across the room, to a portrait of Jesus Christ.

I had just finished an interview with an absolutely poor man and his wife, yet I was unmoved by their plight. I was about to go when the rooster stirred and my host asked if I'd like to see it. That's when I felt the tug. There, across the warped linoleum, the rooster began to scavenge and pose, drawing me back to a time thirty-five years ago when I played among chickens, chased them, fed them, watched them die, often ate them. I was six, living with my grandmother and two great-aunts on the outskirts of El Paso, Texas. I thought everyone had chickens; they seemed more common, more *heard* than cats or dogs. And a rooster's crow at dawn simply meant, Everything's okay, you can wake up now. For me, a first-grader at Ascarate Elementary School, that magnificent, gut-holding screech was as gentle as the Schubert "Ave Maria" soothingly delivered by radio every afternoon as prelude to the most delicious siestas of my life.

Nowadays I still take naps when I can, and occasionally I think I can feel an adobe-cooled breeze reach me across the years

here in California. But I never see live, running-around chickens any more—that is, unless I'm in a Mexican neighborhood,
and even then they're always outdoors. (The last time I saw
livestock indoors was years ago doing Peace Corps duty in
Peru.) Yet here I was, practically across the street from some of
the classiest real estate in the world—LA's cluster of new high-
rising banks and hotels—watching a rooster exercise in someone's living room; at the same time, I was ducking to avoid a
pigeon's low passes. "He only hits the wall," my host said gin-
gerly, more worried about the rooster messing on the floor than
me being impaled on a bird's beak.

Moments later, the rooster was placed under his crate and I
said good-bye. Amparo, my host, waved from the entrance of
the shabby, three-story apartment house. I drove off, on to
interview more poor people in apartments, in clinics, in soup
lines, and along the tracks and freeways leading out of and into
Los Angeles.

Of all these people, Amparo; her husband, Julio; and their six
children probably were the most pitiable of the lot. At least they
gave every reason to evoke pity—yet I felt none. Instead, I felt
something else.

Admittedly their case is unusual. Ten years ago they entered
Southern California illegally from Mexico. For six years they
worked in a sort of take-out slaughterhouse. From pens contain-
ing goats, beef cattle, sheep, hogs, and poultry, customers would
pick out animals, explain how they wanted the meat cut, and
within minutes workmen would have it neatly sliced, wrapped,
and ready to go. Julio—tall, strong, and intelligent—soon became the dynamo and foreman of the operation, which did so
well that his crew hardly could keep up with the orders for
parties, weddings, and restaurants. For her part, Amparo—
which means "help" in Spanish—became head cook and laun-
dress of the workers, most of whom were from her hometown in
the state of Jalisco. In return, the owner of the slaughterhouse
gave the family its meals and shelter in addition to Julio's salary
of eighty dollars a week.

One night, in a moment of carelessness, Julio brought disaster
on them all: he broke his neck. He had driven his old Plymouth
around a corner too fast, hit a curb, and the jolt snapped his

spinal cord. In an instant he became a lifetime quadriplegic, able to move only his head.

Since that time, four years ago, most of Julio's relatives have returned to Mexico, and the owner has closed the slaughterhouse. Helpless, Julio became a ward of the California and LA County medical systems. For a year and a half he lived on a respirator and was provided with recuperative therapy. Several times he was released but readmitted after developing complications. One time he almost died in a county hospital—from "neglect," Amparo explained, not complaining but stating the record. He had several bedsores the size of her fist, "open, down to the bone," and here she drew back the sheet so I could see the monstrous scars and stitch lines left after the operation in which a chunk of his calf was put into the hole that had been one yawning sore in his thigh.

"They didn't turn him," Amparo said. "I would have to sneak into the hospital and do the turning myself." Amparo also described her husband's cracked, white lips. "I asked the nurse why she didn't give him water, and she said that the glass of water was right there by his table, right in front of his eyes. 'But he can't move his hands,' I said. And she just acted as if it wasn't her fault he was paralyzed."

Julio survived the hospital ordeal only to present his wife with the job of caring for a full-time complete-care patient. "I do everything for him." She mentioned this in passing while talking about a new and cheaper kind of adult-size disposable diaper. That is, changing him and catching his urine at various times throughout the day are automatic, unquestioned duties for her, much the same as feeding her children or braiding the hair of her three girls.

At first, Medi-Cal and the state's disability insurance helped them buy supplies and pay for medical attention. However, now, under new regulations, Julio has no medical benefits, leaving him and his family mostly dependent on some two hundred dollars a month from disability. Also, Amparo cannot work, because she must be with Julio (he still uses a respirator occasionally), and they are long overdue on their monthly, $325 rent payments.

But that's not all. Like any modern-day Dickens tale, these

woes are minor when compared with the real dragon in their future: deportation. "What will happen if you're sent back to Mexico?" I asked Julio.

"I'll die." There was nothing hidden behind the tone; he meant only that since assistance and money-making prospects would be virtually nonexistent, death in Mexico would be a certainty. Julio, somehow tall even in bed, gestured with a tilt of his head, as if picking out steers for slaughter, ordering his men to grab this one or that one. "I'll die."

Amparo explained that at one time they could have received "green card" work-permit visas. They had applied for the visas years ago and essentially had only to sign some papers and pick up the visas at the U.S. consulate in Guadalajara. They were about to do this when Julio broke his neck. "Two years went by before I could think of anything else," she added. "Now it's too late. But I'll keep trying."

"Trying" means that if the Immigration and Naturalization Service agents come knocking before the landlord evicts them, they'll try to use their American-born youngest child as a kind of immigration toehold. Nothing is certain, though, until this year's new immigration laws become clear.

Meanwhile, Amparo, like the boxed-in rooster, lets herself out of the apartment only a few times a day, never away from Julio for long and always watchful for *la migra,* those uniformed women and men whose job it is to remove and repatriate illegally entered immigrants. "I used to be timid," she said. "Before the accident, I was the quiet one. I let my husband do all the talking. He made the decisions. Now I do everything. I talk things over with him, but I do everything." Amparo mentioned this as if she were surprising herself with such an admission. And I think there was pride in her voice. Then she swept her hand over her hair, which was pulled back and gathered tightly behind; it was showing gray, maybe too early for a woman in her middle thirties (her eldest child is in high school). While the interview went on, she moved constantly—bringing me coffee, showing a neighbor some dress material bought for her in Tijuana, massaging Julio, putting a glass of water to his lips, and most often selling candies, little caramel and lemon-drop, paper-wrapped, end-twisted candies, to a relentless gathering of preschoolers, all apartment-house children. One after another, the tiny hands would open like flowers, and Amparo would pluck out the pennies, nickels, and dimes, then drop the goodies in each hand. A coffee cup on the dresser by her husband's bed served as cash register. She appeared to count the coins again as she deposited each one. "Pennies pay for bread," she said, smiling.

The room, Julio's room, was crowded. Behind me was another tall dresser crowned with an old television. He doesn't watch much, she said, because it's all the same—"same people, same stories." His kids, though, come in to watch, and in this way his world becomes a place for visits, for talk, even for worship. Christ, two saints, and the Virgin of Guadalupe look on from the walls and shelves. A priest comes now and then to hear confession; if Julio could finger his rosary beads, which hang from his bed, he would. Calendars, posters, and pictures also hang near the bed, and everywhere, it seems, boxes, bottles, and paper shopping bags have been neatly tucked or stacked.

Off to one side, behind a faded curtain that covers the closet entrance, someone moaned. From beneath the curtain, partly covered by a blanket, an arm appeared, slender, brown, decorated with a tiny gold-colored chain. Amparo explained that the girl—actually a young woman—slept during the day in the closet because she cleaned offices during the night.

At the time of the interview, this cataloguing of details was a reporter's reflex; it was almost a distraction, a time passer, a way to say I was "catching" poverty. Years ago I used to fall into the same habit while reporting on the poor in Latin America. I also wondered why I had none of the missionary's zeal, no ideology for fighting inequality or righting wrongs. And while I still have problems with this, I do know that I frequently felt an empathy born not of pity but of a common experience, one which in my case was rooted in those rural Texas times I spent as a child. Somehow I've never trusted the easy emotions aroused by the sight of beggars, invalids, the jobless, the homeless, even the hungry. Perhaps it's because such emotions are so short-lived, do not reach deep enough, do not touch our common origins as people, our common destiny as the bones and dust we become.

So I waited. Amparo and Julio told me their stories, showed

me the pictures of their children, especially the snapshot of the
eldest girl marching with chin and chest out, leading her
school's drill team. I continued to wait. I would not force truth
here, would not pry into something as private as how people
cope with misfortune. If sympathy or insight would come, it
would come. As I said at the outset, nothing deep, nothing that
touched my stem of emotions and memories, occurred until
that leggy, scrawny rooster freed my mind.

Suddenly Amparo could easily have been my wise and tough
great-aunt Concha, or my other aunt, Pema, the tender one. Or
the decisive decision maker, my grandmother Julia. But it was
Concha whom Amparo most resembled. As I remember, Concha had brown-stained, callused fingers. In one hand she could
roll her own cigarettes and pull the drawstring of the little
tobacco pouch, and with the other hand she could pinch off the
match flame with thumb and forefinger. And she was forever
busy, storing her bottles and boxes, counting her pennies, sew-
ing, knitting, gardening.

Concha and her two sisters, like Amparo, were ranch women
who came north to wash floors, cook, and clean for others. They
knew about cattle, about hides, about butchering, about birds in
the kitchen. They could joke about death one day, and the next
day they could start mourning in black for months. I remember
the men, too, vaguely—they were mostly strong-willed, wind-
hardened fellows with boots and blocked hats, men from the
steppes of Chihuahua, laconic, used to hardship and disappointment. You might say stoic.

Julio, in his way, is also stoic, hardly a *chillón,* or crybaby.
What he has endured without much complaint reminds me of
the toughest characters created by that supreme storyteller
Juan Rulfo (stories collected in *El llano en llamas,* or *The Burning Plain.)* No heroes in the usual sense, these men of the dry,
hot Jalisco basin face all sorts of tragedy: hunger, illness,
drought, grand deceit, and violence both savage and slow. They
suffer and don't always triumph, as Julio in his case may not.
However, Rulfo's men and women bespeak a greater triumph,
one of collective perseverance, which is nothing less than a
bedrock of plain, practical common sense. No illusions and very
few dreams.

"In the hospital," Julio said, "I saw others try to kill themselves. I wanted to stop them, but I couldn't. So I yelled and yelled, and the nurse finally came to stop them. One man tried to kill himself twice, one time by hanging himself on some tubes and another time by not using the respirator." Julio paused and shook his head. "Poor guys. They were thinking thoughts they shouldn't think. If you're never going to walk, then you should never think of yourself walking. You have to forget it. I know what happens. You can go crazy thinking about things you can't do."

In Mexico there's a saying, "Tell me how you die and I'll tell you who you are." In the United States the emphasis is reversed: "Tell me how you lived [that is, your deeds] and I'll tell you who you are." If Julio saw suicide as a coward's way out, he didn't say; but he was saddened that those men had so little comfort, perhaps so little love, in their lives. When he told me about those near-suicides, he seemed to imply that if you face illness, injury, and even death with courage, head on, then you can live or die at peace with yourself and those around you. There is also a sense of wholeness, of pride in your existence.

For too long, Mexico has had the reputation of being a nation obsessed with death: harsh, Spanish roots; the removal of one religion of sacrifice for another; revolutions; bullfights; Days of the Dead; the images trail on in countless stories and films. What is usually overlooked is the equally strong Mexican emphasis on life-giving, creative forces. A familiarity with death, as the poet Octavio Paz would say, is the reverse of an obsession with life; together they form a duality that should not be torn apart.

I mention death here because Julio and all the other truly poor are palpably closer to physical deterioration and death than most of the nonpoor. They are the ones closer to hunger, sickness, and mental depression. They have no choice about contending with adversity; they must do battle or go down. In this regard, Julio, Amparo, and most of the Mexican immigrants I've known—including my two sets of grandparents—have been toughened realists, survivors or else.

As it turns out, with a harsh yet understandable logic, these people are usually the last to be considered for government assistance. This, I believe, is unfortunate, because Julio and Amparo—and by cultural extension all the poorer Latin Americans entering the United States—actually provide America with a human treasure that affirms life, tenaciously. The so-called immigrant, pioneering spirit should be esteemed, and not only by employers with piles of dirty dishes.

Julio and his family may be bused out tomorrow, straight to Mexicali, or flown to Guadalajara and released. But if they leave, we lose. We lose his teenaged daughter who intends to join the Army, we lose a boy who wants to study electronics, and we lose a wife who has rallied her neighbors to improve the conditions of their dilapidated neighborhood. Most of all, we lose a family of strong traditions and certain innate beliefs about human closeness, human concerns—all of which are a rare contribution to our world of ciphers and machines.

Julio would like to work again, helped by prosthesis and computers; he knows it can be done; he has seen it in the hospital. But of course it takes money. He told me this directly, without hesitation, as if it could be true, as if someday he would just get around to it. Right now he will be patient. As it is, he doesn't even use his wheelchair, which stands folded up in a corner, a convenient hanging spot for clothes. The chair, he explained, is too big for the room, in a way, too big for the apartment, because there's so little space to maneuver it around.

Although a gritty fatalism pervades the typical Juan Rulfo story, it seemed to me that Julio and Amparo had left behind them that side of their origins. In the stories, men and women face hardship with an apparent indifference; and what might be seen as passive acceptance is actually a jeer, a challenge that taunts fate to do its worst. These characters of rural Mexico, in order to survive centuries of subjugation, have taken on a kind of "what the hell, let's get it over with" attitude. By contrast, Julio and Amparo appear to have kept their toughness and realism intact; at the same time, they have been changed by the opportunities found in the United States. They have become cautious optimists—even now, with all their setbacks, they are slightly optimistic. Maybe they're foolish, but they can't seem to discard hope. As long as there's work, most things in life are possible: marriage, kids, a house, education, on and on. Taxes and citizenship are also part of the picture; and if it doesn't happen in this generation, it will happen in the next.

Over three generations my own family has had its share of successes and failures. Ambitious schemes would flop, and the defeated could try again and again. Those chickens I chased in Texas, for example, ran through the skeletal barn stalls of one of my grandfather's first ventures, a dairy farm, which prospered and died. Then there was his part ownership in an oil well that went dry. Then came a truck service between El Paso and Los Angeles; that business got stuck in the sand somewhere in the California deserts. Other relatives may not have been as ambitious as my grandfather—they were everything from messcooks to movie extras—but at least they tried; they had a few dreams.

Julio, too, has a modest dream. Once again he wants to oversee a slaughterhouse. He said that as long as he can see, speak, and think, it's a possibility. "There's so much to do, and I know how to do it. All I need are the people and the chance."

Sometimes I hear the comment that the illegal immigrant poor are better off here than they would be in Latin America, that they ought to be thankful they're here and not expect handouts. Yes, generally they are better off. However, what most observers of the immigrant scene overlook are some of the serious psychological trade-offs that occur when people emigrate. These trade-offs, or changes in behavior, are intangible and cannot be counted.

What happens is that families eventually give up a big part of their culture: their language, their ways of raising children, their traditional sense of time, their sense of pleasure, even their sense of human closeness, human warmth are all sacrificed in the pursuit of survival and success. Psychologically, America exacts its price from these newcomers. For instance, a Dominican "juice-squeezer" in a Manhattan health-food take-out told me he's afraid his children will see the world as one giant clock insatiably fed by dollar bills. "There's got to be more to life than that," he said. Another immigrant, a mulatto woman from the Caribbean, said she grew up thinking the word *negra*—or black —was an affectionate word; then, in San Francisco, during her first week in the United States she discovered hatred could also power such a word. And in Washington, D.C., a Salvadoran janitor told me that what bothers him most is that Americans refuse to get involved with people. "They say hi and they smile a lot," he explained, "but their eyes and minds are somewhere else. They keep you at a distance."

These kinds of comments are seldom voiced to nonimmigrants, for who wants to appear ungrateful? Newcomers simply try to adjust, get along, as they always have. And for most Americans this psychological change facing immigrants is easy to ignore, because it's invisible. Walking into that little apartment, there in the shadow of towering banks and oil companies, I certainly couldn't see the change, that loss of place and culture. It was too subtle for the eyes. Julio and Amparo weren't about to help me, either, by complaining.

As I said, I didn't see the change until I saw it in myself. Spurred by two generations of Americanization, I had learned to run like a clock, say hi a lot, catalogue details about people, notice rosaries, saints, scars, even touch the grime on broken windows. I could also shake hands and say good-bye efficiently, smoothly, eager to return to my less crowded, newer, and cleaner world.

But I hadn't figured on that rooster.

At the Heart of All Poverty

DAVID RAY

IT'S TRUE THAT I HAVEN'T DONE QUITE THE ASSIGNMENT WE discussed.

I wanted to do a more metaphysical examination of poverty and how it *feels,* let that be document enough. My definition is a broad one, for poverty, like other evils, is the fallout of ignorance; not the gift of the gods, but of men. That is the Platonic view, but our leaders—if they study the past at all—prefer Thrasymachus, who thought might makes right, and Antiphon, who thought justice was whatever is expedient. There's such an immense poverty at the top, under the top hats, and stone hearts wobble under the silk pinstripes. And so we abuse and neglect one another and defer our important decisions to fools or machines. Once one has suffered this poverty of the thirties or of the eighties (which make the thirties look like the nuclear-free paradise of Eden) its hurt is felt always. The sufferings of its children are forever the barometers of a society's ignorance.

from a letter to the editors accompanying his work—

1.

Who would dare translate him back
to sharecropper, father of woes, mound
of red earth marked with tin, reed in the wind?
Grandfather, our Robert E. Lee, victor over rock
in the great Wilderness, General of melons,
onions, forger of his own iron plow and wheel,
he stood in gray dignity, flood at his feet,
weeds for his crops, staunch in his business
of losses. A gentleman, bearded like Lee,
grizzly, his saber a hoe, his mount
a gray mule, his campaign in truth
a great Wilderness. His medals were brass
buttons of overalls. He's in bronze, upright
on horseback, his tomb gilt-doored, nobly
pillared. Stained glass could tell
the stations of his life, the walk
from Tennessee, the hardship farming, wife
dead in childbirth, those rough years
of the Depression, the flivver sold
and all dignity like flotsam of a flood
gone quickly, nor does that river turn,
bring back. By my time all sign was gone
of the good life lost. He spat
tobacco past me before he hitched that mule
to plow the worthless acres. His stub hand
held a melon like a world, turned it.

2.

What it was like—
rain on the tin roof
salvaged from a powerhouse—
the children underfoot
father fretful over fields
being washed away
each raindrop a bullet
killing off his farm.
Earth bleeds away,
gift to the roiling
creek. From the back
window he could see
over the tops of trees
on that steep hillslope
the last-plowed field.
Static on the radio,
mule kicking at a stump.
He was not a man
to stay inside, would run
through spiderwebs until
he dropped and darkness won.
He could never tell her—
He prayed for war.

3.

When the young husband was late from the town
Some vague fear kept her looking
Up at the sky, at the twinkling stars.
She hugged herself, shivered. And then
He came crackling through the brush, a bear
Of a man, drunk, without a greeting.
She'd watch him till she saw
Just what he needed, hoped
He'd wait until the children slept.
They never spoke as man and wife now.
A mule brayed behind the wooden fence.
Her greeting was nothing but a sigh
And yet she took his hand and led him in
As soon as he had relieved himself in weeds
Just like a mule, swaying in the moonlight.
And after love she stared
At the open flame, fire tulip
In the center of the floor, oil waste
Throbbing from earth's hard stone ribs.
The children whimpered and she shushed them.

4.

If I returned I'd brush aside
webs of spiders strung, fuzzing
the road where my mother ran
out screaming, bearing her girl child
bleeding, and I'd tromp down barbed wire
thorned, kick planks that walled us in.
Weeds grow there, waist-high,
though cows graze paths and I step
into shadows, roofless, where their love
made me, staved-in cave, and sun
on ancient bedsprings rusting,
fifty years of rain, red earth failing,
while men of true achievement
invented woe for millions.

5.

I don't believe in modern times, I believe in those times.
Still the heartbreak, no sign of the sea.
Still the child in the arms, bare feet, bewildered
Look away from the sun.
I have not gone forward into years of light.
I have fallen back into those years.
For the touch of those arms I would have to go backward
Face by face, arm by arm, through a thousand failures.
Why not start at the beginning, with the first sadness?

6.

A cellar would keep jars cool.
He promised to dig one.
He could dig one with a mule
And a piece of iron.
But first he had to break the mule
And that was a mean business.
But he kept his vow
And later the mule
Ran away, flipping the iron
Of the scraper end over end
Frightening the boy
Like everything else
The young man and the mule did.
And she bore jars into the damp earth
Like a Cretan girl.
She placed the jars
Upon shelves that are fallen,
All broken
In this Agamemnon's tomb.
And I, the boy, have come to dig
Shards out of the wet leaves
And find what they left.
Here are the rusty cans
Our mother fed us from
When she denied the breast,
Small dugs that I remember,
With nipples like dark figs.
Here are the rusty springs
Of our bed, both brother
And sister.
And here is a rusty ring
Like a half-moon,
Basin she washed us in,
Our little bodies glistening
In candlelight.
You were indeed the most cursed
Of parents, *genitori*,

The rains hurt at your house
And at last washed it away.
And the open flame in the middle
Of your dirt floor
Burned at your bed
Like a rich man's eyes, deep pools
Of oil.
In the day you went out and broke
Stones. The mule learned
To turn away
From the ruins, salt stains on earth.
And stunned by your own failure
Christ's life ago, you left
The gates wide open, iron gates.

7.

A man and a woman were up here
in the hills.
They broke rocks.
They broke each other.
They made of the scrub oak
a labyrinth
for finding the bleached bone
of a cow, a pelvis.
And yellow daisies grow,
as over a battlefield.

8.

A flush toilet was an item in magazines
or the Sears Roebuck catalogue, the one
W.T. stayed up late at night studying,
under the coal-oil lamp, thinking how Ada
could use a new corset or cookstove
or even one of those porcelain flush toilets.
Meanwhile we trudged to the outhouse
where last year's catalogue was sharp as a knife.
And we worried about the black widow
down in the shadows, spider that had bitten
W.T. so that he had run out into the night,
flailing about like a fool, with his pants down.
On such a farm there were no refrigerators,
and the lights were still gas lamps on the wall
with white mantles like little knitted cones.
We ate possums, greens, cornbread and milk,
salt pork, beans, and tomatoes and squash,
melons from the fields. White, denatured
bread was just coming in, wrapped in waxed paper,
Wonder, or Rainbow. On the Fourth, uncles
drank home brew while we ate red watermelon
the same way the black people did, running
it across our faces and spitting out the seeds
at the hungry dogs. Altogether I would say
the quality of life was better back in Eden.

9.

The one-room school was two miles
on red dust snaking through hills.
We returned to find Ada, blue
smoke of her Maytag sputtering away,
puffs striking the smokehouse, white goose
at her feet, then her clothes
on the line, dripping on grass near the well,
bucket tipped up, tied with wet rope.
Those clothes would smell of ash always
from that soap she made in her kettle,
black with little feet like pigs' ears,
spraddling her sticks that licked
colorless flame in the wind—Ada
patient and whiskered, hair
in a bun we never saw down, woman
Grandfather wooed through the mails,
hearing a widow was left with two kids.
He sent her a snapshot of four-year-old
Bea, on the back wrote with a pencil,
"This is my little girl, and the chikens."
She wrote, "I've got two, that makes seven
we kin raise." She came on the train,
Ada whose smile always broke
with her tears, whose biscuits were soft
as a breast unloosed, hot at the face.

10.

We find her on a side street
of Sapulpa, living
in a little tomb her son
built of stones.
We walk in, under
the catalpa tree, and
she cradles our faces
in her hands,
asking where we've been.
"I'll cook for you-uns," she says,
knowing we came for the old days,
knowing we can see reflected
in her eyes
the clock and the daybed
and the fields through
the window, with cousins
stooping there.
In the front bedroom, where
she slept with Grampa,
the dog with the chipped ear
listens.
The stove blazes through isinglass.
We have found for a moment
this woman with her hair
in a bun, who stood with Grampa
before a giant wooden wheel
that went nowhere
while we hopped round like chickens.

11.

After we moved into Mounds
and the duplex apartment while father
barbered (and then the procession
of foster homes courtesy Welfare Department
capped at last by the orphanage),
she served in white shoes the rich man,
owner of a factory stamping steel
or weaving baskets made of wire.
She tucked his three children in, read them
bedtime stories, loved them as her own.
And when she came to see us
Sundays in the orphanage,
she wept and asked that we recall
her virtues, how the night we moved
the final time, she scrubbed floors
till they glowed like glass.
Of course we well remembered. She had worked
till midnight, on her knees.
She showed us snapshots. In one
she held rich baby up, beside his carriage
while two girls stood in fur coats squinting,
darlings, and she was a proud mother again
in a uniform, all white as snow.
Those Sundays when she left anew
we'd run back upstairs, look out to see
her walk away, snow-white feet past roses
red and blurred inside a circling wall of brick.

12.

Speaking of the Thirties
you recall those spirits
frail and insubstantial
who haunted garbage pails.
And a white cat named Snowball,
and dirigibles
like the Hindenburg
and the classic cartoons
whose words hang over you still—
I'M HUNGRY or APPLES, FIVE CENTS.
You speak of those spirits
as if they're out of El Greco,
thin as smoke, rising
into gray skies, taking the earth
with them, like funneling twisters.
In your mind you place the hobo
lifting the trash can
in a scene, the white cat
Snowball standing by him
in the alley lined with rusty barrels,
and the dirigible floating above,
all in black and white like a dream
and Hitler dancing, goose-stepping,
playing with fire,
and all the fathers trembling.

13.

There's a ghost that lingers.
Be quiet if you want to hear
that migrant voice distinctly
or even watch it move. You must
be indolent almost, give up
your own fond clutch
of what you are. The ghosts
come home, this migrant mother,
barber father, all their daughters
grown so fat now
outside their house trailers,
a kind of fête champêtre
years overdue. This fellowship
is comfort on a day when years
lie row by row so tamely
one on one they seem to fall
like pages of a folio, thin leaves
of gold against black earth
once open for the gift of seed.

14.

A humble man, he stands
beside his chair,
his own hair needing trim.
He wears a plaid wool jacket for
his shop front has no door.
On a hook above the half-silvered
mirror, a talcum brush and clippers
touch his profiled head, Aztec
I think. He's got an oil can,
radio, and Testament. The cup
and tiny pot are both for tea,
no tequila unless I read him wrong.
In Spanish we get through
how many years I have and children and
how I like the temperate *clima*
and how my father was a barber too.
The cold enamel chair he touches
with oxblood leather on its arms
is not the one my father
shoved against for years,
circled like a Samson at his millstone,
and moved from town to town. Once it sat
high on a truck of junk, was splashed
with midnight rain while mother wept
in dashboard light and father drove.
The landlord chased us with a gun.
Nor am I still the boy of wounded eyes
who when the trade was slow
climbed up to sit on a crooked crate,
a mannikin for practice trims.
On father's wall a picture hung
of Long Hair Custer, in blue shirt,
white collar stars, red strangling kerchief.
He made his last stand on his knees
with pistol raised while all around him
the yelping braves took scalps.
He had come to murder, stayed to die.

15.

As a Buddhist tried for months
to visualize a small gold Bodhisattva on the air
I benignly conjure up this couple,
his arms about her, free of trouble.
They're young and smiling, apple clean,
whose embraces gave my shining hair,
and she is both his piano and his cello,
which are played with fingers, light
arpeggios now and then, rough gutsy
rubbing of the belly when it's night.
And how well I know, in cold December,
the poor lived better, in glowing embers
of their kindling crates than we did
wrapped in our clawed-up gramma's quilts.
In the decades later they still obsess us
so that daily we forgive them and daily
don't, and in a field may find them still,
blue in paired flowers, their love transposed
and borne beyond a billion rocks, and time,
or they're caught within a cave by those
who knew them before us, suffering sister,
who wept in the Oklahoma night,
And I smile to see our mother still,
cradling the steaming soup, straight down
the hill, to the wretched poor who huddled there
while we at home, brother, sister, sucked the bloody air.

16.

The toys I stole were not from the rich,
but from the poor who lived by the ditch
along the railroad track, in a gray tin warehouse.
They may well have found those toys
on the cold concrete floor when they moved in
with their crates and rags and broken chairs,
but profligate and careless, they had left
some of my favorites out in the high weeds—
a blue Shirley Temple dish was the bowl
in which they fed their dog, who was friendly.
That was the first toy I stole from them.
Call it a toy—I played with it, hid it,
along with the cap pistol and the dolls
and the wonderful miniature tin pump
with little buckets tied to a chain,
water for horses, perhaps, on a ranch.
Three of us were peeing in it in our hideout
when my mother caught us, confiscated
all our stolen toys and made me return them
with painful apologies to the dozen
poor children of the fat lady in rags.
She made me kneel to the dog,
tell him how sorry I was. Truly
I was sorry, though the dog licked my face
and began again to slurp water
from the beautiful blue bowl that had
Shirley Temple's face and curls in the bottom.
And later my father whipped me too
and for a week they both humiliated me with words,
for stealing the toys, for peeing in one,
for not feeling sorry for those poorer than poor,
poorer than we were. After that, I stole from the rich.

17.

In that maimed, befogged and accursed year,
'29, our gas shut off, grandmother
gave birth to twins. She died, but they lived
in a drawer for a week. Many like Laocoön
failed to break the python's hold; it twisted
tight as hell round yet another family.
Beefsteak was out; inland we ate greens
and quail, squirrels and possum, tree bark.
But Al Smith worked his last erection up,
tall zenith from the black-hole nadir of that year,
light-catching scraper of the clouds, in stone.
Brave workers sat mile-high to have their cup
of Thermos tea, knees above a dream's abyss,
and down below an apple saved a wretched man
who had labored making cars till they let him go.
And this year the lady on the bus
says her benefits are cut. She has to give
half her pittance to the doctor, half for heat.
And how, she asks, can a lady live on nothing?
Her black, moth-eaten gloves remind me
of how they've found such holes in brains, work
of insects of despair and tiny predatory birds of wrath.

18.

In the Bosch painting
wind blows rags
from where it
suffers,
makes blood
splash loud.
Garments slash
about.
Watching skies
we see
nether ends
of woe,
such grief and
never a scream.
We name names.

19.

When Mother had married again
and took us back from the orphans
and we moved into town
to live in a streetcar on blocks
behind the tavern, in shadows
of stored beer cartons, I found
that the town needed me,
desperately.
At first I just gave them the news.
Then I slid on the iced rails
of streetcars, with their food,
then their mail, anything special.
Summer I dished stew
down at the Oasis Grill and Poolhall,
then emptied the slop, passing
by billiards and snooker. In smoke
was a man with one eye, lost the other
fighting in Spain, the Lincoln Brigade.
Afternoons he sat on the curb,
spooking the school-kids, though that side
of the street was forbidden them.
The town needed me to mow
the church and the cemetery. I swept
green hair off stone, dirt off names.
It's a wonder I didn't build that town.
They kept a small boy running.
But I return and there's still
no town built there
nor anyone sowing the seeds
of *Communitas*
on the right side of the tracks.
But I cross over and stare
where chickens peck
at the ruins of black Myrtle's shack.
At dawn each day, with glistening chest,
she took her letter, signed my slate,
and I wondered who could love her,

to write her daily, pay for stamps.
White folks had less love, I thought,
or were shy with words. As I rode
my bike through mud and ice I thought and thought.

20.

Johnny Mack, my friend and hated enemy,
for the privilege of walking you to school
I'd wait half an hour, slobber
while you ate your steaming breakfast, served
by your Aunt Vesta, whose huge soft bosom
you bragged you saw each time
she took her pink bra off.
I hated you, my only friend,
still envy your complacent monkey's
smile, buck teeth, and your refusal
to be taken in. Just once I thought
I'd found out something first, and bragged,
pointing to the sky, "Those are cumulus!"
But you promptly shot me down:
"You just got that out of *True Comics,*
I saw it first!" Again and again
you won all argument, cut me down
in that trash-burning town
till I began to think that you
and not those faces overseas
were the Japanese enemy. (They too
had buck teeth, short black clipped hair.)
We tied for the high I.Q., the teacher
had to tell us so we'd fight.
Locked horns, scraped knees, eyes
gouged, hair pulled out on Elm Street
and then again between the jungle bars at school.
And all the while I thought
quite clearly, calmly, of those hot
breakfasts your aunt who loved you
served, ignoring me, lifting in devotion
the golden egg, the plate of toast, the gleaming
jam. Against my bitter shore
I felt backlashing wash, high churning waves
of envy, tides of salt. She hugged you tight,
till you were lost in her, caught
in softness, squirming, and those magic

loaves neglected. How I stood and hungered,
longed to rush forward, for that love you spurned.
At night, defeated, I'd disappear
behind your yellow house and boxrow hedges
topped with snow like doilies scattered
and in our room above your chill garage
open up a box of Kraft half-dinner,
heat the yellow goo for me and Sis
while we thought of mother
who nursed the dying bed by bed.

21.

Just once he gave me a dime
as he came out of the house
back to argue again,
back to glance at us briefly.
Stopped in the yard and looked down
at his boy, and dug in his pocket.
"You be good, you hear," as if the dime
would buy devotion for life.
I touched and retouched that thin dime,
after his car had gone small,
whispered over and over, "Mine."
Those who have nothing give nothing.
Those with a dime give a dime.

22.

In India the peasants hack
at anything that's growing
and live beside the railroad tracks
in their huts of rust and tin.
In Kansas City the hobo pulls
his cardboard cover up
and rests his head on a rubber tire,
strums in smoggy air
      his imaginary guitar.

23.

At the crowded Ganges once I hitched a ride
with tour-group tourists in their bus—
They'd let me join them for that trip
to the airport through seven miles of city,
more of countryside. The members of that group
wore wide-brimmed straws, sipped Cokes
they'd brought along, showed each other
trinkets they had bargained for, flutes,
jade, bronze, sarees, bamboo back scratchers,
sandalwood and camphor, carved figures they had
no idea were gods. They had checked out
of the five-star hotel with the fine swimming pool
at dawn to see the river, all
that pageantry of craziness, monks
in prayer, girls bathing, cremation fires,
and all along they obeyed injunctions
not to touch or taste. And now through glass
I saw the world as they had seen it always.
Out in the fields the peasants looked
like tableaux in museums. On lovely heads
that bobbed along, the ladies lifted firewood.
Men in diaper dhotis plowed dry earth
while bare, redundant children ran everywhere
and below our tinted windows on a busy
roadside trail a horde was fleeing war.
Their bodies gleamed from what was surely heat.
I had to guess, for in that air-conditioned air
I felt no sense of heat and dust. The scene
outside might well have been a movie. That's how
we see the world now, from air-conditioned rooms,
from bombers ten miles high. Yet now and then
above that music, humming tires, or through
the aëry entrails streaming
across the poisoned sky, a voice gets through,
our leader singing of his loves, the merchant kings,
the royal, the famous, justly idle.
And he tells us of his hates, the welfare

cheaters, cripples, hungry kids, blight
upon our landscape. And he smiles to think
of beauty bare—the shiny missiles, rockets,
vats of poison gas, pits of peril, glowing pools
of woe, debt to bind the ages. I heard him,
in those twangy tones from home, that tour-group
horde, and thought of Gandhi too, whose voice
rose up in heat and dust: "I saw the tears
of the oppressed." Two voices, contrapuntal.

24.

Not that his politics were on the Right,
but that he thought a kingship would be kinder.
Blood shed to shatter shackles and reweld them
struck him as a waste. He dreamed
of queens and if a beauty was no queen,
he mused, slave quarters also lent
gilding light to cotton beds, or straw.
He fought no battles, for the war
was lost in peace invariably, that follows
triumph for every noble notion. He liked to speak
of India, the mess they made themselves
when the ugly Raj was soundly exiled,
and our Civil War that gave the Blacks
their freedom to hammer in the din of assembly lines
or nurse their welfare babies in our tenements.
In fact, he had a briefcase of examples
I closed my ears to while I thought of noble causes,
one after another. We all know what they are
and how they need their cups of blood.
The cup is sweet, he mocked,
                    if you're the God who drinks it.

25.

I cursed when I got there early,
that little airport far from the town,
cursed and set my bags down as if stranded
for far more than an hour, and in worse weather.
But then I walked out, down the tar road,
across it and into a field sloping off
toward a blue valley. The mud ruts gleamed
and a cottontail ran in dun grass.
Through this valley, I knew, Lee's
graycoats had marched, seeking
out battle, invading. And the dry
leaves were already bronze, unconcerned.
Now a nuclear plant broods, just over
the next hill, sending its clouds
to the sky, the deep growl of its atoms
ripping apart infinitesimal bit by bit
our rock of the earth, subtle as sex,
as private, interior, perilous,
stitching, unstitching, tying the bonds
of life and of death, fire linking fire,
and the chill birds sang me their music.
My grief floated off, and I walked
in my blue coat like one of those
who live in the forest, friend even to man.

26.

The young girl paying with food stamps
holds the U.S. Department of Agriculture booklet
while the cashier rips coupons out, counts them
like cash. This with the girl's right hand.
Her left is busy with the baby,
tucked underarm like a sack of potatoes,
babe watching me carefully, sapphire eyes
alert, curious in his snowsuit. And the mother's
mother awaits her at end
of this checkout line as if
we've arrived on a plane. Her eyes are expectant;
She'll rush to embrace all arrivals.
(Few feel so fortunate, blessed
with life on a Friday, with rain on the way,
possibly snow.) Then she carries across
the tar lot the sacks with the milk
and bread and cheese and peanut butter,
three generations, the oldest gone to fat
in fuchsia slacks, happy
to walk beside her daughter, share
this babe of wonder, doll
for the high school years. And the girl
is lovely, angel-haired, good
lover I am sure. I imagine her in candlelight,
with lithe legs, small breasts that nursed.
And the babe is cute with luminous eyes
like sapphires and I have noted
she bought no cigarettes or beer,
good girl, eyes clear
on life's necessities. The three
soon are stuffed in an old orange Pinto,
off on life's errands. The babe
alone looks back on me, eyes
like blue marbles I flicked in alleys.

27.

It's been six, maybe seven years now
since Mrs. Webster had her sale, estate
sale, most of what she owned
(I bought the stereopticon and luggage).
And now, out beyond the edge of town
we stop in heat and have our meal
near Blue Arch Village, and I wonder
if she's there, if it was much
of a disappointment, living without
the things she once lived with, if she lies
awake at night counting missing china
or gold and silver frames she gave up
to let her fading photos sprawl in drawers.
As we leave the Burger King, I glance
at the Arch old people's home, a sordid
stucco suburb where, cajoled to play
shuffleboard and not to think too much,
they're herded, rounded up from cities,
installed in two-room kitchenettes
and sold the burial and health plan
and given a weekly ride in a painted-over
school bus to a ballgame or a church,
but never, never back to the old neighborhood.
And over the city are scattered
those items haggled for in the sales,
the splendid Venetian glass, the round
oak table, the Kabuki doll from the trip,
honeymoon or vows renewed. And they know,
the least of them, the rules: that no
neighbor will inquire after them, even
when stopping so near, on the highway,
that no greed will spare what is left,
a few fond relics, no ethic bring back
the silver dollar left by accident
in the oaken Singer's drawer. They are wise
enough to know that even next of kin

will make off with what they can. And when
I travel I carry the middle-sized rattan
suitcase, with prewar craftsmanship,
              worth clinging tight to.

28.

This strangeness aglow, we watch a man
descend into a submarine, crash-dive again,
and he's been dead for twenty years. We fall
in love with some image of a woman dancing
(serving up a head upon a tray),
and she's been dead and in her grave
for thirty (and the hero cut his throat
in Barcelona, and his costar
like a twin of the heavens
died miserably of drugs). But still,
her breast is soft and falls
into our hands. In shadows we gaze
toward the only center, light, await
a common fate, mushrooming fire
from which these gods alone will be exempt,
flames sent to gather curling faces, lovers
we have felt so deeply, never touched,
and uncles who became our presidents.

29.

The gray-stubbled man who sleeps
in the abandoned car, wrapped
in his army coat from Goodwill,
curls in the front seat
clutching his throat, hearing
his teeth, hoping they will think
of him, those who pray
for the chances of each
delicate life, how they want
even the little fish of a person
to survive and to prosper.
That's it, he thinks in the night,
when he lies still and stares
at the dashboard, black holes
inside shadows, the next life, that's it,
being in the womb, safe and sound,
cared about, argued for, everyone
wanting to help, curled knees to chin.
He thinks of the sea and of the womb
and he thinks of the bomb brooding
and hunger because it is on him, rat
gnawing. And he wonders if in an earlier
incarnation he was a soldier
trying to sleep just before the fight
at Chickamauga or Spotsylvania.
He's sure he can almost remember
being killed, falling after the sword-slash.
And he thinks of the women like bread loaves
and how he has nothing, not one of the loaves.
In the next life! he thinks, drops a tear,
and remembers the name of his mother.

30.

A man of the past, printer trained
in his trade, linotyper gone from town
to town seeking work, flotsam
turned up in the South amidst oaks
and magnolias, Confederate flags still
in front of motels where he cannot rest
or say through the phone, "You come too."
Seekers get nothing, not food stamps,
only the face paralytic, cold eye repeated.
He heads home, there to be licensed to beg.
All he owns he shoves in a cart, wire
net from Safeway, black wheels. A dog
trots beside him, friend needing friend.
Home by dark? Hardly, but dark is a home.

31.

The graph of infant deaths is etching
out our grapes of wrath,
and there's woe in rain and snow,
while our President decries
the corporate tax.

32.

DOING WITHOUT
    's an interesting
custom, involving such in-
    visible items as the food
that's not on the table, the clothes
    that are not on the back,
the radio whose only music
    is silence. Doing without
is a great protector of reputations
    since all places one cannot go
are fabulous, and only the rare and
    enlightened plowman in his field
or on his mountain does not overrate
    what he does not or cannot have.
Saluting through their windows
    of cathedral glass those restaurants
we must not enter (unless like burglars
    we become subject to arrest)
we greet with our twinkling eyes
    the faces of others who do
without, the lady with the fishing
    pole, and the man who looks
amused because he's found
    another piece of firewood.

33.

HAVING TOO MUCH
  shows in more places, not
only the face but the belly
  and the polished leather. Wher-
ever you go, round every port
  of call, folks who practice
this custom walk with cameras
  knocking their knees
and genitals. Like busybodies
  they have so many friends
to look in on they can never
  quite catch up. They must use
boats, planes, rockets, upon
  which they distribute
cigarettes like tickets
  that will glow and take you
anywhere, even to the moon
  or death when it opens
up for the season. What they
  have learned is certain lessons
which they are fond of citing,
  e.g., *money talks*, and they appear
to be in despair
  from never absorbing quite
enough electricity.

34.

There's a song, "Take Me Back to Tulsa,"
one of my father's favorites,
and I am, at last, taken back to Tulsa,
to a banquet in my honor,
in a fine hotel with gilded mirrors
and red velvet drapes, where darky waiters
light the candles by our steaks.
I'm king of the orphans, and given a seat
with the others who survived, who learned
how to smile, to hide the fire
of bitterness burning still in the eyes.
And we are there with survivors
of other sad scenes, some of them worse,
far worse, and we hate ourselves
because we survived and did not go through
the worst. We look around and realize
that all this elegance, mirrors, kindness,
oil-rich families regarding lobster
as lunch-meat, all was here, when tears
on my face wet the flat pillow and I looked
toward these buildings, the fine hotel
and the skyscraper floodlit with rainbows.
No one brought me in to eat, then.
No one asked me how I felt.
The pillows of the beds were damp all night
all across that room of bunks. I heard
boys whimper far into the night, call out
sometimes, "Pa" or "Ma" or "Mom" or "Sis,"
and the floodlights on stone we stared at
changed their colors till the dawn
and I recalled how on the farm we all drank
from the same dipper made from a hollowed gourd
and how once I went with Dad
to sell melons we had grown (he'd beaten me
for hoeing some instead of weeds). And I thought
of visiting Sundays when no one came,
and of the rich folks who were escorted through

like tourists, adolescent girls in furs
gawking at us while we washed,
a dozen naked in a shower. And at night
we heard the tom-tom drums of those
who crouched in valleys, hugged their hills.

35.

I fell asleep thinking of our astronaut,
how thrilled he was, rolling
in the skies as in the womb, free,
unfrightened, loving his umbilical
cord, fondling it, then walking
across the moon, taking gold
mountains away from the poets.
In school,
The little backs hunched there helpless
look like a picture on an old postcard,
sepia, forlorn, children of the prairies,
babes of the foolish immigrants
who brought their innocence and hopes.
I watch the one who has no pride,
looks as if he'll rise and step
forward, looking at us, to ask for more.

36.

Fifty years after the Thirties
I find them anew, mother with sister,
holding her, up late in the rocker,
safe from the scurrying rats.
A candle of pig fat glows from a corner.
Outside in dark the flood swirls.
Grandfather claws at salt earth,
grows melons snubbed in the town.
Sundays we sing hymns in the church
where bats hang from high rafters.
Skies bring black twisters, dust storms,
so we flee back to the cellars.
But cows did not tremble with tumors
And the sun was not feared as father of bombs.

37.

As a child I watched the hobo in the alley.
Today he sorts the Farmers' Market trash.
That same tomato breaks against the face.

38.

In Mamallapuram by the sea you saw
half-naked men dig in the shells
of peanuts tossed in mud.
They searched through each one,
already cleaned out, would lick
even a thin, papery red skin.
You saw that, my daughters, in India,
something I once saw in America
while dirigibles floated in blue skies
of the Thirties, when we boys
burned Hitler in our trash barrels
when alleys were crowded with hoboes,
men bending, stooping, searching.
And you saw a blind beggar
speaking Tamil, begging of another,
who turned up his face, pointing
to his own eyes, saying, "Friend,
I am one of you." Then another
led him toward us, foreigners
who would be his salvation,
and he showed us the gaping wounds
of his eyes. I took you halfway
round our globe for that,
not for the world's greatest
bas-relief, elephant in granite
slipping down mountains to the Ganges,
but for those beggars, so you might see them,
believe them, know how it was,
how it will be, our eyes burning like fire,
our wounds gaping and red and accusing.

39.

Smudgepots,
called that because they smudge
the sky, even the stratosphere,
threaten to crack us all
wide open, melt
the floating glaciers
and joined all to all
consummate the so-called
greenhouse effect, turn Manhattan
into Venice, gondolas
long-poled searching canyon floors,
docking at the top floors only.
And all so trivial, these bright
and tiny tongues of fire, orange
like Van Gogh daisies.
It took a bunch
to drive him mad, a field
full, bitterly and heavily full
of the brightness, the burning.

40.

For days we forget
the world is not as it was.
We ignore the sign for shelter,
the arrow pointing to hell,
and the siren that's practiced
for years, for Armageddon.
For weeks at a time we eat
and make love, forgetting
that day will come when there may be
no time at all to enter the underground,
to enswathe ourselves with others
in cocoons of our fear and blankets
archaic as sheep, no time to say
what we need so desperately to say.
And for whole months the world seems
like the Thirties—no progress at all.
The hungry still whine.
Slums seek revenge, babes
cower in corners, big fish
eat little fish, welfare rats
welfare babies, death by fire
and the bribed inspector. And the soup
kitchen, at back of a station wagon
looking like that scene of West Tulsa
when I rode Uncle Henry's shoulder,
clung to his hair and we both stooped
through the doorway, man and boy humbled,
bending over the long plank
of the table, as do convicts in prison,
blowing the soup to cool it, lifting the bowl,
furtively looking about. And the children
in school, eyes bombed out by T.V., drugs
cheaper than love, chant *ashes ashes*
we all fall down, like Daddy at the Die-in.
When we're old enough to think, they think,
we'll all be dead.

41.

When I went back to the orphanage
and saw my playmates of yore
or others just like them,
nothing was changed, though Donald
was gone, whose gramma
had brought him all she could spare—
a shiny red apple, a *delicious,*
for Christmas. And Mary Lou,
my first love, who held hands
under the table, had vanished,
married, mothering, if she survived
the years of the Girls' Home.
And strolling like a sergeant inspecting,
I observed the small faces closely,
no expression at all as they watched,
pale as sycamore bark. I asked one
why he was there, and he shrugged.
(His parents still lived, as mine had.)
"Do you hear from them?" "No."
"Do you know where they are?" "No."
"What will you do when you grow up?"
He had shrugs for every occasion,
and I saw he had not learned how to smile.
But I did not blame him, and had
nothing to give but a blank
wounded expression, and an apple.

*Poverty in America is not merely economic. I have seen it among
the wealthy: a mind-set of hunger, deprivation, touchy greedi-
ness, of a persistent and grieving conviction that one has been
cheated and that a vindictive and mean attitude toward the
world is a justified response, a clinging to some belief (perhaps
based on childhood slight) that the world's priorities are so
wrongheaded that they will never be set right. And possibly
that is the case.*

*There is the poverty suffered by the have-nots, but there is
also the excruciating poverty of those who are afraid to give,*

who are locked into lovelessness, and who do not know when to leave things alone: air, land, water, other cultures. It is always easier to solve the problems of others than of ourselves, and we commit much evil with such do-gooding, when in truth we need to look to the curing of ourselves. (I am not voicing isolationism; we could help abroad, too, but perhaps with food and condoms, rather than random machine-gun fire from our helicopters.) My view is Platonic, of course: Plato insisted that evil derives from ignorance. If we knew the right thing to do, presumably we would do it; and therefore we are victims of misinformation. I think of the programming of violence and indifference in the media and in our schools, but I also think of the fashions, how the children of the prosperous are narrowed as persons by being told to avoid poverty, to close their eyes to suffering.

Economic wrongs are taproots, but if postwar prosperity taught anything, it is that without a persistent examination of values, economic resources are merely the freedom to burden the world with waste, to tool the economy for weaponry that's restless to be used, and to suffer boredom in a society that lacks purpose and in fact envies other cultures despite their economic deprivation, because they have purpose and vision.

We can't decide what to do with our unwanted children, and yet the drawing boards are busy with interplanetary schemes and wars based on video game scenarios. We can't stop smog but go along with costly preparations for an Armageddon so certain that the men who once pranced with signs on their backs denouncing the end of the world are no longer cartoon figures. Our despair, our numbness, and our poverty—not only economic—can hardly be chronicled. In my poem I have tried to express some of the sadness those barometers of poverty, our children, are made to carry with them as a life sentence. As Kuprin once said, "The horror is that there is no horror."

It's Very Hard to Say I'm Poor.

MAXINE KUMIN

IN THE CONVERTED ATTIC OF THE OLD CLAPBOARD HOUSE
where thirty-nine-year-old Carla Sanderson (not her real name)
rents a second-floor apartment for one half of her $718 monthly
take-home pay, her little boy keeps a white rat with boudoir-
pink eyes in a cage. Its bedding of pine shavings is fresh, the
water dish is clean, there are food pellets in the miniature bowl.
The rat's name is Lester and he is tame enough to handle, a fact
that ten-year-old Paul demonstrates by taking him out and en-
couraging him to crawl up his shirt.

Julie, the daughter, has a kitten which is at that rangy stage
when the legs look too long for the body. Carla is worried that
the kitten may be pregnant, having recently gotten loose two
days in a row. Feeding three children, one kitten, and one rat on
food stamps and a stringently budgeted salary may be possible,
if not highly plausible, but a litter of kittens, or the bill for
neutering the cat, would create still another financial crisis in a
life peppered with them.

The baby of the family, a blond three-year-old juggernaut
named Nicholas, tugs his one-armed highchair across the
kitchen floor to use as a stepladder. In seconds he's up on the
counter, reaching for a bottle of soap-bubble liquid.

The family's three chairs are all in the kitchen. This makes an
awkward situation on the evening of my visit. As Carla and I
attempt to have a conversation, the two older children vie for
the remaining seat. Supper, it turns out, hasn't been served.
Gradually the reason becomes apparent. There's nothing in the
house to eat except a package of frozen waffles. The November
food stamps didn't arrive in the mail, although this is the sixth
day of the month. Grudgingly the kids settle down to eat what
they scornfully label breakfast food. The main course is toasted

waffles and tap water. For dessert, some applesauce I brought, along with a batch of homemade cookies. I hadn't thought to pack the pot of soup now simmering on my stove, twenty miles away. Rather, I *had* thought of it, but I hadn't wanted to come on like Lady Bountiful, with all that might imply about Carla's inability to provide for the family she is so fiercely and agilely bringing up alone.

I muse a minute on frozen waffles, something I classify, with fast food in general, as tasteless, uneconomical, and minimally nutritious. On the other hand, where is the spare half hour in this mother's hectic schedule to devise the wholesome, upper-middle-class batter with wheat germ stirred in for extra protein?

The terrible irony of holding a household together on little better than the minimum wage is that Carla can never amass any savings to buy items on sale. She can't afford to order a case of frozen orange juice to take advantage of the bulk price. No half a side of beef for the freezer, at a bargain rate. No bargains. The poor are at the mercy of gougers. The only grocery stores that will extend credit until the next paycheck are corner shops that have to charge much more than the chains in order to make a profit. So it's a vicious circle; it's frozen waffles and water for Friday-night supper instead of roast chicken and cranberry sauce.

Of course, one reason for Carla's financial problems is that she spends too much on housing. But she is determined to stay on this quiet street. Her apartment in this blue-collar neighborhood is far better than the ramshackle, unheatable place she started out in. There, she had to contend with transients and drifters. Here, people plant petunias in their front yards and obediently put out their trash barrels on pickup days. The district's elementary school is considered one of the best in the city. It's worth the struggle to make ends meet—not that they ever do—to be able to stay here.

Poverty American style doesn't announce itself in rags and tatters. The first time I met Carla she was wearing a plaid skirt, a white blouse, a tan vest and the comfortable People's Republic of China cotton shoes that have become the preferred footwear of a generation of young American women. The variety of relatively inexpensive, mass-produced ready-to-wear clothes, and the ease with which the middle class discards and replaces its garments, make "Outgrown" shops and "One-More-Time" boutiques meccas for people like Carla Sanderson. Good used items for kids are not so easy to come by. For one thing, outgrown clothing gets handed on, even in affluent families. For another, kids are notoriously hard on their clothes. Nothing about Carla's attire hints that she is below the official poverty level—the single parent of three children, willing to enter into hand-to-hand combat with the bureaucracy to ensure them a decent upbringing.

Carla has a secretarial job with a municipal agency in this New England town. Although I call it a town, with its comfortable, three-buckboards-abreast Main Street crisscrossed by seven or eight side streets, and farmland around the edges, it's actually a city. Much of what Carla does from eight-thirty to five involves meeting the public, providing information about city and state agencies, and channeling complaints and requests to the proper doorway of City Hall. She impressed me that first day as a calm, efficient, attractive daughter of the middle class, a picture hard to reconcile with her impassioned letter to a women's group, printed in a newsletter that had crossed my desk a few weeks earlier.

My own daughter is a single parent in Switzerland, juggling a year-old child and a sensitive job involving political refugees with the exigencies of her private life. Although Swiss social-service agencies provide exceptional day care, and her problems are not compounded by financial difficulties, she, too, suffers from single-parent burnout. She, too, endures the frequent frustration and often bone-chilling loneliness of the life she has chosen. Through her I've become more aware of the desperate problems confronting young women who are going it alone, particularly those in this country who, like Carla, are under the knife of Reaganomics.

But let Carla tell it: "Have you ever been there?" she demanded in her letter. "Have you ever wondered how many more days you can let your child go to school in stormy weather with shoes that are torn apart and you simply do not have the money to buy new ones? Have you ever used your food-stamp change to buy toilet paper, or get one load of wash done? [Such purchases are illegal under the food-stamp program.] Well, I have—and much more.

"Do you know what it's like to face the coming winter months on $700 a month when your apartment rent and utilities total $365, and you have no winter clothing for your children, and they need shoes, never mind boots? And the Administration says, 'Tighten your belts more, please'—more cuts are coming, probably in food stamps, child nutrition, medical benefits, heating assistance."

Carla has been trapped in one double bind after another. In flight from an alcoholic, abusive spouse in California, she returned to New England with her children a little more than a year ago, when, as she puts it, "I decided it was time to take control of my life again. I sold my possessions, forwarded twenty-seven cartons to relatives, packed two foam mattresses and three children into my station wagon and headed home. I was really feeling adventurous—sort of a reverse pioneer— heading East in *my* wagon. I had never camped out, had never done any long-distance driving. Twelve weary days later we arrived."

Within two weeks she found a job and an apartment, but soon discovered that on a salary of $4.46 an hour she could not quite do it all on her own. Although eligible for day care, she had to choose from a list of sitters approved by the state. But her sitter needed to be paid each week, and the state would not reimburse Carla until after at least three, and possibly as many as twelve, weeks. When Carla remonstrated, she was told, "Maybe you can't *afford* a job right now, honey. Maybe you'll just have to go on welfare."

Nevertheless, she persevered. She found a summer-camp program at the Y and a bus service that would take the two older children directly from school to the day-care center once classes began in September. Her precarious schedule worked. She was almost elated at her newfound ability to cope.

Then, on October 1, 1982, the Reagan budget cuts abolished the bus service and eliminated the $60 a month she received through Aid to Families with Dependent Children. Further Reagan pruning decreed that she was no longer eligible for

Medicaid, because she earned more than $521 per month. That loss was a disaster for Carla. Since she had been hired as a temporary employee, she did not qualify for the medical insurance her employer provided. And with three dependents, coverage was essential. The welfare caseworker was right. She couldn't afford the luxury of a job.

Now that she is a permanent employee, Carla manages without the A.F.D.C. supplement, but she still avails herself of food stamps and day-care assistance. Recently she received a 2 percent raise, but since benefits are calculated on the basis of gross earnings, she faces a 5 percent reduction in food stamps—even though her take-home pay will be reduced 4 percent because of mandatory deductions for a retirement program. No redress for this kind of paradox exists in the system.

A statewide food-stamp heist, meanwhile, is depriving Carla and all other recipients of two weeks' worth of stamps: The date of issue is being pushed back, three days at a time, from the first of the month to the fifteenth, meaning that each month's allocation must last an extra three days. The stamps are not being prorated, and it appears that everyone is expected to stretch her benefits for the next five months while the Administration makes up for what looks suspiciously like a shortfall in funding for the program. That's hard enough for Carla to do—but what about a family with seven or eight children? What about infants and the elderly? How do you tell *them* not to eat?

"Who has the luxury of intellectualizing about the Reagan administration?" Carla asks. "When we do stop to think about it, we realize that the government has morally turned its back on single-parenting women and their families; further, it seems to be shoving our problems under the rug because somehow *we're* immoral. We should be home with our families and not out in the working world. The message seems to be that if the programs are taken away, women will have no choice but to 'stay in their place,' even if the place is a violent battleground.

"During a legislative budget hearing, a state representative who is a Reagan enthusiast said in an aside that he had heard that people facing cuts would be forced back onto, or into, the [welfare] system, and he felt that if they wanted to be *spiteful*, let them. Spiteful! Would it be spite to give up a low-paying position with no medical benefits in order to gain Medicaid for a chronically ill baby? If you cannot get children to after-school day care, can you as a mother keep from wondering what's the sense of working in a dead-end job? Is letting a six-year-old come home from school alone and afraid to an empty house a 'viable alternative'? Our children need and deserve a lot better.

"I'm still from that middle-class upbringing that makes it very hard for me to say that I'm poor," Carla says as we talk across the battered kitchen table. "To accept the truth, I am *poor*. The last week in August we ate oatmeal three times a day because that's what was left in the cupboard; can you believe that?"

If it hadn't been for the WIC vouchers, there might not have been cereal during that critical period in August between the end of summer camp and the start of Carla's new job. Yet WIC —a food-supplement program for women, infants and children up to age five with proven nutritional deficiencies—injects another irony into Carla's life. The program is a direct outgrowth of the Vietnam War. So many recruits were rejected by the armed services because they were physically unfit that a federal program was devised to improve the diets of nutritionally substandard families. As much as one quarter of the population in the rural South is malnourished; the figure is easily that high in some pockets of chronic, severe unemployment elsewhere.

Although Carla would have to be pregnant to be eligible for the program herself, it provides orange juice, certain cereals, and eggs for her youngest child. But the vouchers have only another two months to run, and Nickie, who is the picture of robust good health, will then be deprived of these high-protein treats. Carla may reapply for the grant in six months. If Nickie is deemed malnourished at that time, the coupons will be reinstated for another six months. Another paradox in a nation with a mountain of surplus butter slowly going rancid, with warehouses chock-full of dried milk solids and cheese aging to the point of no return.

Still, Carla is quick to point out that she is luckier than most women in her situation. She has some job skills; she has a start on a college education: two years of credits. She has ambitions to complete a degree in human services at a local college. At the moment, this is unthinkable. Even if she received a Pell grant, which is not considered income, she would also need a student loan, which is, and which would put her over the maximum level at which she would qualify for day care and food stamps. Once again, she can't *afford* the luxury, this time the luxury of a loan that would enable her to improve her skills and move up the economic ladder far from these pitiful entitlements.

Entitlements—benefits people qualify for on grounds of age, occupation, or income—are not synonymous with welfare, although programs like A.F.D.C., WIC, food stamps, and so on fall within the entitlements budget. But only about 17 percent of that budget is spent on so-called "means-tested" allotments—or aid to the poor. The total outlay for A.F.D.C., the program the new conservatives are most likely to attack as subject to the most fraud and abuse, constitutes about one third of the money paid out for civil service pensions. Military retirement pay costs the federal government 1.3 times as much as its total outlay for the food-stamp program. (See James Fallows' November 1982 articles in *The Atlantic* for chapter and verse.)

Carla is outraged by the bureaucracy's unwillingness or inability to pursue delinquent fathers. "It is against the law *not* to support your children, but 80 percent of the divorced fathers are breaking *the* law," she declares. Many men who owe child support claim to be unemployed while holding jobs that pay them under the table. Carla feels that a substantial number of them see this as a kind of vengeance. "But women are somehow made to feel guilty" for the failure of their former husbands to provide even minimal monthly payments.

"I don't know what else will happen this winter," Carla says. "I don't know what else *can* happen. Last year we managed to stay warm, thanks to the federal heating-assistance grant. This year there are going to be more cuts—maybe I won't be eligible. Right now, I don't want to know. It takes all my energy juggling this." She gestures at the three jack-o'-lanterns she carved out of pumpkins a local farmer gave her for the children the day before Halloween. "I couldn't justify buying them, and he had a fieldful he said he had no use for."

The sweep of her arm takes in Lester the rat and Nicely the kitten. The gesture encompasses Nickie's day-care finger paintings taped to the refrigerator; the letter Julie received from the

United Way thanking her for her one-dollar contribution, which the child proudly brought out for my inspection; the snapshots of all three children neatly framed and hanging on the wall; the philodendron plants hanging in Carla's bedroom; the surplus army cots arranged as an L-shaped couch and covered with a floral-patterned spread in the living room.

Carla is hanging on, barely, in a system that is stacked against her. There is little room in her life for recreation or socializing. Weekends are given over to marking time in the laundromat, attending Paul's soccer games, getting everyone off to church and Sunday school.

Would she like to meet a good man, fall in love, remarry? Right now, Carla says, "It's doubtful. I feel that for eight years I stayed in abusive situations out of feelings of powerlessness. I thought I deserved what I got, that I wasn't good enough, that wanting anything for myself was selfish. Now I'm independent; I'm making a life for my kids. So my singlehood—or celibacy, if you want to be accurate—is a trade-off."

She says she is frequently scared, angry, and depressed, but she's a scrapper. She will battle the bureaucracy for her missing food stamps, she will wear out shoe leather campaigning for sympathetic candidates for public office. She is articulate, creative, and passionately maternal.

"What do I want for my kids? How do you answer *that* in twenty-five words or less! I want them to have a chance, to explore doing the things they're good at: Paul, his flair for acting; Julie, her gymnastics." She pauses, shaking her head. "But those are only the externals. I want them to be kind and aware, to add something to the world as they grow up."

I balance Carla's staunch optimism against the ukases of Reaganomics: less and less for more and more people. As the little they receive is taken from them, it will be harder for Carla's kids to add something. And the more harshly society treats its Carla Sandersons, the deeper each one of us is driven into a spiritual wilderness.

My piece about Carla Sanderson arose quite naturally out of my response to an open letter from her which appeared in the newsletter of the New Hampshire Commission on the Status of

*Women. An intermediary brought us together. I did nothing
except restate Carla's story for a larger audience.*

*What amazed me was the quantity of mail generated by
publication of this little article. Two responses may be worth
mentioning, as they represent two polarities. The fourteen-year-
old prep-school son of a friend in affluent suburbia was sure the
article was fiction; else how could he handle the obtrusiveness
of such inequities between his life and Paul Sanderson's? And
an elderly gentleman in another part of the country sent a $150
box of nonperishable foodstuffs to Carla. I sensed from his
letters that he could ill afford to do so.*

Meanwhile, plus ça change, plus ç'est la même chose. . . .
*Carla says in a letter to me that "you've made me sound braver
than I am." Every month she performs the same cliff-hanging
feat to stretch food stamps across the gap of children's appe-
tites. Since I've been dividing my modest remunerations for the
article with Carla, she's been able to buy a battery for her
flagging car. Now that the articles are coming out in book form,
she'll have some new tires.*

Out of Work and Out of Sight

JOHN VAN DER ZEE

THE WOMAN CARRYING THE BASKET STACKED CHIN-HIGH with her belongings is being escorted from the apartment by a cop. As a group of children from the surrounding apartments sit their bikes to watch, the officer follows her across the courtyard, a patchy combination of dandelions and bare earth, once a lawn.

"You better not go back to him!" howls the young man who has come out of the apartment after her. He has dark hair and mustache and is wearing a white T-shirt, red shorts, and no shoes. Tendons in his neck stand out as he shouts.

"Fuck you!" the woman bellows back over her shoulder, her voice echoing off the walls of the apartment complex, sound waves engulfing a neighbor stoicly headed out with her laundry and the absorbed kids on their bikes as if they are all trapped inside a giant speaker. The officer leads the woman with the basket beyond the courtyard to the facing street outside.

From the street, the apartment complex resembles its architect's dream: handsomely landscaped, determinedly modern, on a wide, clean boulevard lined with shade trees and splashed with summer sunshine. Troubled times and troubled people have made it into something else. Rents are going up, while jobs and public assistance are going down, in Fremont, California, where people without prospects of jobs or shelter move in together to avoid the streets. Two nights before, in this same complex, two women had a fistfight. The previous week there was a suicide. Every night there is an argument.

Over the past two years, there have been thirteen plant closings in this area—Pacific States Steel, Caterpillar, Hunt-Wesson, Peterbilt—capped by the shutdown, in March of 1982, of a GM assembly plant which, at its peak, had employed six thousand people.

A few blocks away from the apartment complex, four burly men stand restlessly in the atrium of the Fremont office of the state of California's Employment Development Department. Wearing jeans, sport shirts, thick-soled shoes, they look out of place standing on floral shopping-mall carpet instead of a factory floor, with a background of Muzak instead of a forklift's whine.

Shunted from office to office, where they are given tests and advice about how to conduct themselves in job interviews and encouraged to exchange information, they are anxious for the shared sense of work.

"The story you hear other places is all the same," says a man who puts one foot up on the tiled planter that forms the centerpiece of the atrium. " 'We've got people on layoff and we're not hiring anybody new.' "

"I had to multiply fractions," a man in his forties says of his test. "I've forgotten how to multiply fractions."

The atrium is busy, with men like themselves going in and out of rooms.

"How'd it go?"

"No runs, no hits, three errors."

"—and nobody left on."

"All they can say is no."

"Have you seen," says one of the men, in a German accent, "at the Orchard Supply, they have an electronic stud-finder? A quite beautiful piece of machinery, with lights all in a row? It's on sale now."

"My father could find them just by pounding the wall," says one of the other men.

"It's great if it works," says a third man, who begins thumping his fist around on the hallway walls, searching for a solid construction stud.

Suddenly all the men are trying it, bending over, stretching up, moving up and down the employment-office hall, letting out little yelps of satisfaction when they come on something solid, finding release at last in something approximating the exercise of craft.

As with an increasing number of major and minor family dislocations in Fremont and the adjoining cities of Union City and Newark, some aspect of both these situations will most likely wind up on the doorstep of an office in the back of a school on a quiet residential street, the headquarters of Tri-City Volunteers, Inc., the local last resort for the hungry, the homeless, the battered, and the suicidal. In a time of the most alarming unemployment totals in local history, when more than a dozen county agencies have been cut back for lack of funds, the cries of the needy and the desperate are constant.

"Demand has increased every month," says Mary Hewitt, Tri-City's director. "There has always been hunger in Fremont, but it wasn't visible. Not apparent. Now it's your friends, my friends, our relatives." During the previous month, the center fed five hundred and eighty-five families.

Yet hardship is still not obvious in Fremont, a California miracle city born of incorporation and easily graded growing land, raised on low-interest, low-down-payment housing, and a positive attitude toward industry. Instead of the sooty brick factories of a decaying community with street corners populated by idle men, this is unemployment of a new sort: Its harshness is concealed, its isolation is intensified by the new buildings, the miles of tree-lined streets, the shopping malls, the industrial parks with Choice Space Available and Townhouses for Attractive Terms. What could pass at first glance for a boom is the shuddering inertia that follows a sudden halt.

"The workers who came here had little or no education," says Mary Hewitt. "Often they came from Oakland or from the South. They had grown up with nothing, and were given large salaries for the first time in their lives. GM employed husbands and wives. People bought homes, bought GM cars; then, all of a sudden, it's over. Where do you put someone who's done one thing for seven, ten years—paint a stripe or put on a fender? Now both of them are out, houses to take care of, where do you go? What do you do?"

For a while there was GM assistance and unemployment, but workers with the shortest benefits were the first to be laid off. There are the houses, difficult to sell at recent interest rates, and nearly impossible with the second and third mortgages com-

mon among plant and factory workers in Fremont. Opportunities for other jobs are rare: a local man who started a car wash
has a stack of employment applications as thick as a good-sized
book. And there are always the rumors: GM is going partners
with Toyota, GM is going to start a new production line for mini-
vans; if you apply for another job, they'll make you promise not
to go back if GM starts hiring again.

"Some people go elsewhere, get another job, get laid off, then
come back here and have nothing."

Off the road and off the line they come, out of the bar across
from the GM plant, sometimes from other cities and other
states, come to find work in California, and there is none. They
come out of cars where they've been sleeping, sometimes
whole families, from supermarket parking lots and sometimes
the bushes around the lake in the Fremont Community Park,
desperate, sometimes angry, sometimes faint or weeping,
young women often pregnant, men carrying tots. They come in
big GM cars, they come on buses. One man walked ten miles
from the welfare office in Hayward. People come on motorcy-
cles, on bikes; sometimes they can barely carry the things
they've come here to get: food, canned goods, clothing, utensils,
mattresses, sheets.

It's a situation that can't be solved: the best one can do is cope.

"You have to make up your mind not to try to save everybody
in the world. You do the best you can."

In September of 1981, Mary Hewitt was as much a part of the
boom times here as she is now of the bad. Both she and her
husband were licensed real estate brokers in a city with one of
the most dramatic growth rates in the United States. Indeed,
Fremont is still projected one day to be one of the largest cities
in America. On quiet weekdays, on busy weekends and evenings, she drove Fremont's calm, verdant streets, past its malls
and office complexes, gliding by modern buildings broadly
spaced on an exuberantly expansionist scale, showing its roomy,
landscaped houses to radiantly optimistic families, some of
whom she has since provided with emergency food. Vigorous,
talkative, resourceful, no-nonsense, a grandmother, it is easy to
see in her now the successful salesperson she was then. Like

almost all her customers, she had come to California from some-
place else, Illinois in her case, and had bought a house in the
city's older Niles district, where oldtime movie stars, among
them Broncho Billy Anderson and Charlie Chaplin, had once
made films.

But there was, even then, an ingrained, familial social con-
cern, a take-charge sense of community centered around the
Hewitts' Congregational church, a belief that a good part of the
world operates on assumed responsibility and that people don't
really know what they are capable of doing until they try.
Through her church, as board chairman of Tri-City, Mary Hewitt helped oversee the fund-raisers, stage the garage sales and
gather the clothing on which the organization depends.

She stands at a cluttered desk in a cluttered room, carrying on
a running conversation while at the same time fluctuating between overseeing the individual requests and form-filling by
the hardship cases at the counter, and responding to repeated
telephone referrals of additional people from the county social
welfare bureau.

"We get county food once a month, what's called the Food
Coalition. You have to be applying for welfare help to get this. If
you're not applying, we buy Supplementary Food, three days'
emergency supply. We get six hundred dollars a month from
the county to spend on this, and the churches make up the
extra. The county says they have no money. We're on a one-year
contract, which is now on a three-month extension.

"People have been good about making donations. I don't
know what we'd do without the Congregational church.
Safeway gives us excess bread and desserts. The manager of
Lucky helps me, gives me dents. We give away doughnuts that
the bakeries don't sell. But times are tough for stores, too. They
buy less, so there are fewer extras. Eggs and milk, supermarkets
don't order in quantity any more. If there's too much spoilage,
the manager is gone. In three days, we're out of food."

The director is one of three salaried employees at Tri-City.
The others are a young staff worker whose wife works with him
as a volunteer, and the Center's accountant. The rest of the
workers—drivers, handymen, stock and clerical personnel—
come from the General Grant for State Assistance, charity cases

themselves, who are required to work twelve and a half hours a week in exchange for food, or people sent by the local courts to avoid paying fines or going to jail.

"We need to be open Saturdays, but I don't have the people to do it. People forget. Some have other jobs. Some have learning disabilities, have never found a job, don't know how to work. I'll take them when other people won't.

"We had four ladies, funded by CETA, who were in-home health-care aids. They had files of clients. They kept people out of convalescent hospitals. We lost them when we lost CETA. CETA was costly for some agencies; it didn't pay administrative costs. But, for us, nothing has ever taken its place. Now we must get fifty calls a week for someone who can do cleaning, 'help my mother do her wash, cook for her, take her out once in a while—she can live alone if she has help.' And we can't get it.

"People frown on funding for salaries. It's the one thing they seem to resent most."

Among the anomalies of this new kind of unemployment, along with the officially denied desperation, the broad, clean, empty streets, and the incongruity of hungry people living in $150,000 houses, is clothing. Fremont is a working-class city without blue collars. Out of a combination of factors—the warm summer climate, the nature of apparel stocked by stores catering to what was an emerging suburban clientele, the inflated price of denim work clothes, the kind of castoffs available in local thrift shops—people walk, wander or sometimes weave into the Center in outfits that make them look like summer tourists, often depriving them of the traditional solidarity and earned dignity of willing labor, and sometimes expressing an insouciance completely contradicting the way they actually look and feel.

"IT'S A GOOD DAY TO HAVE BABIES," declares the T-shirt of a young, pregnant woman standing on the other side of the counter with a referral slip for emergency food. She is the third pregnant woman who's come here for food this morning.

"Women are having kids again," Mary comments as the girl bends with a pencil over the required form, "and they're having them whether they've got men or not. To young girls living

in families where people have moved in together, an AFDC—
Aid for Families with Dependent Children—check is a way out.
The girls figure a baby isn't that hard to take care of. They've
been taking care of babies anyway, why not get a check? Now
we're even getting men whose wives have walked out, leaving
the husband with the kids. Men are applying for AFDC.

"We have women pregnant at sixteen, unmarried, going on
AFDC immediately. And the size of the families sometimes is
enormous. Six children. Eight. Eleven. Many of them come now
from cultures where large families are encouraged. Chicano
families. Asian. What's going to happen to these children? One
day we'll have to pay ten times more in social costs if we don't
feed them now."

A Polynesian-looking woman wearing a T-shirt with Tom Sel-
leck's face on it and in script lettering "Magnum, P.I." comes in,
trailed by four children, all in T-shirts with Hawaiian themes.
She has recently arrived from the islands, with eight children
under the age of ten. Now her house has caught fire and she has
been burned out. The family has nothing. They are given blankets, utensils, clothing, a shopping cart full of food.

"Giving them a double order makes you feel good," says
Claudia, the young volunteer who has loaded the shopping cart.
Claudia and her husband first came to the Center as an emergency case: he had been fired, their furniture had been stolen,
they had three kids to feed. That was several months ago.

"It's much worse now. If we'd had our troubles now, we
couldn't have survived it."

A young, pudgy-looking woman in a red T-shirt is standing at
the counter, talking to Mary Hewitt. The shirt reads, "THIS IS
MY   LOUNGE-AROUND-THE-HOUSE,   DO-NOTHING
T-SHIRT." "Did you hear what she just said?" asks Mary, over-
riding another conversation. " 'I had a dollar to my name. I
haven't eaten for three days, but for day-old bread and peanut
butter. My husband works, we're not on welfare, but he just got
cut down.' "

The people start appearing at eight-fifteen in the morning,
when Mary Hewitt arrives at work. The Center staff eat lunch
at their desks. The women wander in, wearing Levi's, often
with babes in arms, and men in tow. There is no scolding or

recrimination. It's a business transaction, food for paperwork. People are beyond recrimination when they come here. And for every referral there must be a separate, confirming phone call—otherwise people will alter the figures on the referral slip, add family members, increase the clothing allowance, then sell the extra clothing at the flea market.

"We had a man come into our thrift store for his clothing allowance. He took a lot of time in there. Finally one of the women called me. He had taken *eleven* suits. I told him he'd exceeded the allotment and made him put them back. Beneath the eleven suits, we found a roast. He'd lifted it from Safeway.

"The rougher the times get, the rougher the people get. People who've had to survive will survive any way they can. The desperate are best-equipped for survival in this time."

Unlike people in traditionally high-unemployment slums, ghettos or barrios, people in Fremont have no unemployment subculture to sustain them. For them there is no body of experience, no folklore, no nearby examples of people who've already weathered what they're going through, no informed street-wise view about where to go to get food and clothing or find shelter. The pride that has taken them out of the slums and made them cling to the American promise of individual advancement now leaves them isolated, puzzled, angry, and often despondent.

"People who've never been on welfare aren't used to this. They think welfare is something to tide you over, an interruption in your current lifestyle. It hits them as a shock that before you can get welfare you have to sell the boat, sell the grand piano, sell the second car. The first thing that they do is threaten to commit suicide.

"A woman called me who lived in a house on three acres of land. Her husband had left her and her two teenage boys with no money, nothing to eat. It was winter and their power had been turned off. She was threatening to do away with herself. I told her the first thing to do was to send those two boys out on those three acres to cut some wood to heat the house. Then come down here and get some food.

"A man, out of work, committed suicide. He was a Hispanic, who hadn't permitted his wife to do anything, not even learn to drive a car. She didn't know what to do. We got her down here, it turns out she had been a nurse. Now she's working, functioning again.

"We had one man, who used to work here, when he got out of food or money, he'd go in and rob somebody with a knife. He was a sweet man and every bit a gentleman, but he's in prison now.

"The survivists will do anything. Steal from the Center, resell old clothes at the flea market. They'll make it. It's the others you have to worry about, the decent, unprepared people."

With so many people out of work, there is more time spent at home. More drinking among men who were heavy drinkers to begin with, more time spent with children by men whose tolerance for children's company is limited. With no pool hall, no club, this is not the traditional seething caldron of the unemployed. Instead, there are thousands of seething teapots, where the boiling is constricted within the walls of a single house, and the fist traditionally shaken at the bosses or the government or the unfairness of the world is instead often thrown at the nearest member of the worker's own family.

In recent months there have been half a dozen suicides among unemployed men in the Fremont area. Alcoholism is up, as are incidents of child abuse, divorce, broken homes. And the battering of wives is up the most alarmingly of all.

"The center for battered women, SAVE, is also here in the school. What happens is that the police are called to a house where the wife has been beaten. They'll tell her to leave right then. Or the woman will wait till the man is out of the house and leave herself. They come with nothing, often with children, and we have to give them everything. One woman was beaten so badly she wore a scarf around her face, like an Arab veil."

The afternoon is when things go crazy at the Center. Fremont is the only city in the county now offering supplemental food, and the word has spread. Now the people who have been referred from other agencies, the people who have had to walk or wait for buses, or drive from distant towns, the battered women who have waited for a time when their husbands weren't around to duck out of the house, now all these converge on the Center.

"We feed people from Union City, Newark, Hayward—even

Oakland, though we're not supposed to. We've had men stand there at the counter and cry. Women have fainted. We've had women who've gone three days without eating. I don't care how they get here, once they're here."

It is, after all, presumed to be an emergency service. The problem is, with conditions as they are now, the emergency never stops.

Like the well-kept, comfortable houses on the tree-lined streets, and the colorful T-shirts with the incongruously upbeat slogans worn by people climbing in and out of large American cars at the shopping malls, the Fremont General Motors assembly plant is a denial of the conventional imagery of industrial unemployment. Instead of heaped mounds of slag or ore, towering smokestacks, cranes throwing steel against the sky, there is a half-mile-long, low-profile, pastel-gray complex, dotted with small vents and stacks, that looks as if it could serve as the headquarters for one of the high-tech electronics firms in Silicon Valley, directly across San Francisco Bay. Everything is muted, clean, orderly, the parking lot ready to receive cars, the railroad stock in the haulaway yard ready to roll them out; over it all is a vast, anticipatory lull, as if the whole complex were primed, waiting for one mighty main switch to be thrown to start the entire landscape humming again.

Across a divided boulevard, in a building with a red tile roof, a patio, and the accommodative air of a regional insurance-company office in an industrial park, is United Auto Workers Local 1364, stirring today in the warmth of an outside interest it hasn't attracted in months. The California State Assembly has passed an emergency bill extending unemployment benefits up to twenty-six weeks for plant workers enrolled in approved retraining programs. The man who introduced the bill, Assemblyman Bill Lockyer, a Democrat who represents the Fremont area and who is running for state senator, is scheduled to present the bill to his constituents. There is word that he'll be accompanied by California Governor Jerry Brown, now campaigning for the U.S. Senate. So the camera trucks have converged on the local's parking lot, an alphabet soup of TV-station call letters, complementing the meat-and-potatoes pickups and vans of the former GM workers and the bread-and-butter Buicks and Oldses of the local city and county officials.

Inside the local, newsmen and -women, local politicians and union officers now on a volunteer basis stand sipping coffee and eating doughnuts, exchanging gossip, feigning indifference to the cameras and lights. They're upstaged for the present by unemployed auto workers, many of whom are black men, greeting one another with exaggerated slaps and high-fives, jive talk and what's happenin's. There is a man wearing a yachting cap with military stars on it, and several black men in Charlie Pride Stetsons. One black dude is dressed entirely in black and white, with a white cowboy hat, black pants, and a black-and-white jacket with lettering on the back: "BILL JOHNSON *IS* THE BARKING DOG." Another man is drinking wine from a bottle in a paper sack.

"I could tell you half of these people I've fed," says Mary Hewitt.

Julie Rosa is here, the warm, large-hearted woman from the county welfare agency, who calls the Center with referrals for food and clothing maybe twenty times a day, along with her boss, the Social Services Director for Alameda County. Stan Allen is here from the Chamber of Commerce, and Leon Mezzetti, the Mayor of Fremont, who runs the local Volkswagen agency. Even the city supervisor who represents the strong John Birch element in Fremont, is here, sharing the limelight with the people and organizations he has vowed to cut back. Good news is so scarce these days that it must be spread around to include everybody.

According to Roy Bertecelli, the young man in charge of local 1364's job retraining program, about 525 GM workers have already begun retraining. The training is done through local schools and community colleges, and the workers are instructed in a variety of specialties, from electronics to welding, to avoid flooding the employment market. Much of the money for retraining comes from GM, as a provision of the previous union contract. Though the placement record has been good, Bertecelli admits that those workers most easily placed may have already been placed. People who are slower to learn new jobs may find the slack in their new category already taken up

by the time they have qualified. Still, the new bill will help: it
will at least allow men and women to eat and pay bills while
they concentrate on learning a new trade.

With the assurance of familiarity, Mary Hewitt moves across
the patio, into the local's business offices, then back to the still-
growing crowd in the assembly room. She knows everyone by
name, has a friendly word for each of them, and is acutely aware
of whose hands are on the levers of local power. The supervisor,
now standing with the mayor, rumored to have his ear, is the
John Bircher, a bright, articulate man who wants to get rid of
the local human relations bureau and the fair-housing organization. He is one of the reasons why Mary prefers to run Tri-City
with county funding and volunteered money. With the cities
involved, there is an excess of politics as well as of paperwork.
Yet her approach to this remains unideological.

"Personally, I don't care what their politics are, as long as
they help me feed people."

There is a crush toward the door, and the TV cameramen
herd out toward the parking lot. Assemblyman Lockyer has
arrived, and Governor Brown is with him, arriving in the now
famous, flamboyantly austere gubernatorial 1974 Plymouth.
There is a tidal shift of noise and attention outside. Then, in a
cluster of murmurs and bodies and lights, Governor Brown
bursts into the room. He walks across the room and sits at a long
table with a union spokesman, the mayor, and Assemblyman
Lockyer; Brown looks pleased, even eager to be here. He is
running behind in the polls, and he is a man who is strongest on
the attack. He has the focused, attentive look of a candidate
about to dig his spurs into an issue and ride it.

There is a brief, adulatory introduction by the acting union
officer, who says that Governor Brown has come here to sign the
bill, and that he and Bill Lockyer will explain it in fuller detail
than the union man is capable of doing, and that the governor
has done an outstanding job and deserves all our support for the
Senate. He's followed by the mayor, a man not noted for elo-
quence, who rises to the occasion by pointing out that "the
quality of life starts with the job."

Then Brown is on his feet, the bill in one hand, tearing into
the Republican Party and the Administration like a street-cor-

ner orator with his dander up. "We must invest in the skills of people," Brown insists. He says that displaced workers must be retrained. Without a policy to retrain people for the technology of the '80s and '90s, our country will not be able to achieve the productivity we need to keep us competitive with foreign nations.

To do this, he argues, we need management and labor pulling together. "We know what kinds of bombs we have and how competitive the Pentagon is. We have to make sure our people have the skills to keep our economy competitive with other nations."

Job retraining, Brown says, arises out of management and labor agreement, backed by government as represented in this bill. The extension is designed to give people the subsistence to finish job retraining courses. "I still believe that 'Made in America' is the best label in the world.

"With a few new faces in the U.S. Senate, that economy is going to get started again. I don't want to be among those displaced workers."

Much of this is a politician telling people things they want to hear; but before you tell people what they want to hear, you must first determine what that is, a projection requiring a certain empathy and entailing risk. It would be easy to say the wrong thing here, to rabble-rouse, condescend or overpromise, but Brown seems to have caught the tone of the moment exactly, balancing his speech between reality and hopefulness.

He introduces Lockyer, the assemblyman who sponsored the bill, a young, appealingly modest man whom Mary Hewitt says has done a good job representing the district. Lockyer tries to hand Brown credit for the bill, but the governor cuts him off.

"I just sign 'em," says Brown. "This is the guy who works for 'em."

Lockyer makes a brief, low-key statement: "This is the least we can do to get people who want to work back into the market."

Brown signs the bill, then holds it aloft to enthusiastic applause. Warming to the audience, he is back on his feet and at the microphone again:

"The number-one challenge to this nation comes from the

elimination of jobs. By the year 2000 it is predicted that forty million current jobs in this country will no longer exist. This is occurring because of foreign imports and the increased use of robotics."

Our only way to combat this, says Brown, is with new machines and new levels of skills for the people who work those machines.

"We are headed for a disaster. This is a piece of a larger economic game plan that's going to strangle America."

What we need to avoid this, he says, is a coalition of management, labor, and government to make sure that retraining will be in growth centers, and that the talents and skills of the American worker will be upgraded—an alternative to the current administration's economic policy, which Brown summarizes as "economic unilateral disarmament."

The speech is over. As Brown answers questions from the newspaper and television reporters in the room, then leads them outside for filmed, individual statements in the parking lot, there is a spreading sense of satisfaction in the room.

Outside, in the sunshine of another gorgeous summer day, the feeling that anything substantial has been changed quickly dissipates. It's another idle morning of another idle day. Across the boulevard, the GM plant seems not just shut down, but obsolete, outdated before its time, like so many recent American cars. The unemployed men from the union hall are once again off to the bars, the TV sets. If they have the time and the money and the gear, they head out to the nearby hunting and fishing spots in the foothills of the Mount Hamilton range. The weather, the mountains, the trees all seem a conspiracy, a denial of the seriousness of people's plight here.

From inside Mary Hewitt's car, headed back toward the Tri-City Center, the backseat stacked high with collected castoff clothing, Fremont, California, looks once again deceptively prosperous. On the streets are tanned, golden classic California kids, charging about on Moto Cross cycles. Who would believe that there is despair here?

When this is mentioned to Mary Hewitt, she smiles. "You know, about a year and a half ago, my husband, George, and I visited the British Isles. We toured England, Scotland, and Ireland. You know the problems they've had there, inflation worse than ours, ailing industries, 14 percent unemployment. But just to pass through that country, seeing it out the window, you'd think you were in paradise."

It is six months later. Just down the block from the Auto Workers local, four senior UAW members stand around the bed of a pickup truck. The union's parking lot is full. This morning, in an elaborate peace-treaty-like ceremony at the GM plant across the boulevard, the president of GM and the chairman of Toyota agreed to produce a new car in Fremont, a compact, front-wheel-drive model whose engine and drive train will be imported from Japan and fitted into a body stamped and put together here. In response, the union members, unrepresented at the signing, have gathered for an impromptu meeting of their own.

In the local's auditorium, crowded with anxious, restless men and women, there is an air of jittery bravado: shouts, boos, applause, a crowd and speakers reinforcing one another in the righteousness of their own positions.

Outside, however, the tone is different: uncertain, serious, subdued. For weeks there has been speculation about what the new venture in Fremont will mean to the auto industry as a whole, and to the six thousand laid-off local workers in particular. Rumors of antitrust action, the formation of similar joint ventures elsewhere, the renegotiation of wage rates and work rules and seniority have produced a combination of hope and fear likely to be the prevailing atmosphere here for months.

"What was it like over there?" one of the men by the pickup asks a reporter from the press conference. There is, in the eyes of all four men, something stunned, expectant, apprehensive: men who have fifteen to twenty-two years in with GM, with the vulnerability of boys. Told that the announcement included no commitment to the union, that the joint venture would be considered a new company, whose employees would decide for themselves whether they would be union or nonunion, the men grow defensive.

"We're *skilled* workers," one of the men insists.

"I'm a millwright," maintains another.

The plant, they claim, cannot operate without them. Yet in the era of robotics, computers, and new work rules, who knows?

"If they don't honor the seniority of people with twelve to twenty-five years in," warns the first man, "ain't no way that plant is going to open."

Yet the choice here—and the company, the UAW, and the individual workers know it—is not between the old contract with the old pay scale, work rules, and labor force, and a new one. It's between a new contract and none. And remaining after everyone's feelings have been aired, and each side's logic has been acknowledged, is this sobering realization. Where once there were six thousand jobs in Fremont, there will be, at most, by the end of 1984, three thousand. Moreover, Ford Motor Company has announced the closing, in May of 1983, of its nearby assembly plant at Milpitas, adding another twenty-five hundred unemployed people, in the same job categories, to those here.

"We pay more union dues than any other local in the country," says the first man. "I been off work a year and eight months, and I've kept up my dues. Couldn't make it if my wife wasn't working."

"My wife isn't working at all," says the millwright. As he speaks, he is trembling.

Like most other people, I suppose, I have a hand-me-down image of unemployment, an amalgam of Dorothea Lange photographs and James Agee, John Steinbeck, and George Orwell prose, a sense of city sidewalks lined with idle, downcast men, standing hunched, hands in pockets, or slumped in doorways. The men are always waiting; they wear dark clothing, hats or cloth caps; it is always winter, or at least cold and overcast.

The reality in California, where some of the most powerful depression photographs were taken, among men and women some of whom might well be the children of transplanted Okies, is so shockingly different it is difficult to grasp, and temptingly easy for a passerby or a junketeering official to ignore.

After all, how bad can life be for someone living in a modern ranch house on a broad, sunny street, with a recreational vehicle parked in the driveway? Bad to desperate, when there isn't money enough to pay the utility bill to keep the house livable. Or to fill the gas tank of the RV. When the tide has run out and left you stranded with an anchor when what you really need is a raft. Then the house and car become emblems not of fulfillment, but of folly, and the men and women burdened with them, cut off from the traditional sustenance of an anonymous city crowd of people in the same circumstances as themselves, are beset with an inescapably personal sense of failure.

I don't know what the answer is to all this. I do know that a country whose industrial capacity has twice been the deciding factor in world wars and has represented, for the past three decades, the strongest deterrent to a third, which ignores and neglects the people who embody that capacity and does so in the name of national defense, is a country with its priorities sadly reversed.

I also know that the effectiveness of a social organization, like that of an individual, will inevitably be destroyed by a prolonged combination of overwork and lack of sustenance, and that it was due to official interference in what were then considered the natural inequities of society that most of what is unique and admirable about this country originated.

And that clinging to images, even powerful and telling ones like those of hard times of the past, insisting on them to the point of trying to impose them in place of a complex, difficult, or conflicting reality, in order to distance ourselves from it, is a delusion common to most of the forms of madness.

Where Will the Young People Go?

SIMON J. ORTIZ

"I'M IN BUSINESS EDUCATION," SAYS PETE PUTRA, 23, WHO IS from Duck Valley, Nevada now, though originally from Rocky Boy, Montana. "I need a skill I can use, so I can go back to Duck Valley and start a business. That's my goal. Right now, Shoshone and Paiute people have to travel twelve miles to get to a store. If there was a store on the reservation, they wouldn't have to go somewhere else. Businesses in off-reservation towns get all the Indian business, and that Indian money doesn't come back. Secretary [of the Interior James] Watt says that Indian people on reservations should be more self-reliant, but at the same time he says, 'We have to close these schools.' The education we need is here, the education we need in order to be self-reliant."

Tim Linville is from Kayenta, Arizona. He's in electronics, as are quite a number of students at the Southwestern Indian Polytechnic Institute (SIPI). He is twenty-four, speaks very easily as he moves about in the dormitory laundry room where we talk. "Electronics is coming more and more to the reservation. Equipment is operated by electronics, like at the coal mines near Kayenta. Industrial equipment and the electric trains are run by computers and electronics. Even simple tools like wrenches have digital readouts to measure torque. It comes down to electronics; I figured it was the best way to go. I have a wife and we're going to have a kid pretty soon. She's at Dennehotso. It's hard for me to be away from her and the little kid that is coming. SIPI is the only school I could really count on that is relevant to me. I figure the Navajo Government has to be going after more and more computerization if it's going to be efficient and accurate. It's going to have to have people qualified. If a machine breaks down, they should hire their own people to repair it."

In the past, most if not all of the so-called expert tribal technicians were white. Indian tribes had to bring in outside technicians to work with current technology whether it was operating equipment or reading blueprints. SIPI has helped to curtail the habit of overdependency on outside aid. There is nothing inherently wrong with receiving help from whites or the outside, but what is wrong is that too often a dependency develops that is stultifying. A school like SIPI is necessary in order to train people to work in their own communities with the technology currently at hand.

"It helps the morale of your people when you have someone from your own fixing things. It helps to see yourself and your people making money. And it helps to be helping whoever needs help," says Tim.

Several students run noisily through the laundry room, and Pete waits until it quiets down before he starts to tell more about Duck Valley, which is on the Nevada–Idaho border. "The Shoshone and Paiute have a tribal farm. Last year, they waited too long to cut the barley, and they lost money on it. It's a rich valley. Water comes from Wild Horse Dam, which is just off the reservation. Owyhee is a little town, the only one, on the reservation. The farm is run by the tribal government. Duck Valley is ninety miles from the nearest city, which is Elko, to the south. There's only a small town, Mountain City, off the reservation. My cousin owns a gas station on the reservation. He's trying to expand. He tried to borrow money, but the tribal-BIA credit committee wouldn't give him a loan. He went to court and won. But the committee is appealing the case, and my cousin still doesn't have his loan. It seems like they're against him, an Indian who's trying to run a business on the reservation."

Economic matters get kind of complex on Indian reservations. Sometimes the factors are intratribal disputes, petty jealousies even, political favoritism, but there are other factors at work. I'm quite sure that Indian people are not overly paranoid, at least no more than anyone else, but sometimes we think there is a conspiracy to prevent us from developing self-reliance and self-sufficiency. Maybe they—the federal and state governments, corporations, all those very powerful elite who are in political, economic, and social control for now—don't really want us to be self-reliant and self-sufficient. They want us to be dependent upon them always. We sometimes think that. What other reason would Watt and the federal government have for eliminating SIPI if they didn't want Indian people to be crushingly dependent?

Tim doesn't hesitate as he says, "They want to go after the natural resources we have, and they use cutbacks and cutoffs as weapons. They want to keep us separated into different tribal areas so we won't unite. What this school gives us is unity. We understand each other here. You won't find that anywhere else. This is about the only place where I can find this togetherness, this feeling that we are one people trying to struggle for life, to survive.

"Maybe they don't want us to be in one place together, talking to each other, sharing our ideas, making our plans and strategies."

To drive home his last statement, Tim remarks, "That's what they don't want. They don't want us to do that. Because once we get the idea, they think we're going to start a revolution."

We all laugh aloud, our voices and laughter bouncing off the cement walls. The washing machine doesn't work. A dryer door hangs loosely open. A table sits on its side, legs broken. The room could use some good outside sunlight. But our laughter and voices feel good to hear.

David Blackfeather has not said much. Though he smiles and laughs easily enough, he is very serious, almost grave in manner and speech. "They don't want us to be one nation. The U.S. wants to keep controlling us. It got turned around. We were the majority; they were the minority. Now people have a handful of this, a handful of that. People and life got eliminated. At home in Pine Ridge, there's a lot of farming and ranching. The Sioux people are trying to get the Black Hills back; there are a lot of natural resources there. The U.S. is trying to pay the people off with one hundred and twenty-four million dollars, trying to wipe the slate clean. The only way to wipe the slate clean is to return what is ours. One hundred and twenty-four million dollars is nothing. It'd be gone in one year after the lawyers and expenses are paid. That's ridiculous, man. Some say we should become a true sovereign nation, even have border guards. It wouldn't mean that we become an enemy. I think then we can get more economic development going, maybe even help from other nations. We better stand up and say, 'Hey, we're not animals. We have minds, we have emotions, we have judgment, reason; this is us. We have religions and a social system. We have desires and needs. We need education.' "

The announcement was made in late December 1981, by then Secretary of the Interior James Watt, under whose office the Bureau of Indian Affairs (BIA) is located in the federal hierarchy: Funding for SIPI through the Bureau of Indian Affairs would not be included in President Reagan's fiscal year 1982–83 budget. The school would no longer exist after October 1, 1982, and the facilities and campus would be converted into a center for other BIA programs and offices.

SIPI student reactions ranged from dismay to shock to outrage. For most, enrolling at the school was the only opportunity for gaining job training, therefore being able to enter the job market with a fair chance of gaining employment. "I am disappointed that the government doesn't realize that a vocational school is important for Indian people. The education they receive here at SIPI is beneficial to Indian people for their future in the working world," said Rayna Lopez. No words were minced by Lucinda Harris, who said, "I'm really mad, disgusted, and discouraged with the federal government. I take it as being racial and a slap in the face. The people learning here go out and get jobs and will not be standing in welfare lines."

The Indian young people had every right to be angry. They had come from just about every state in the union believing that they could gain employable skills training at SIPI. Most students who come to SIPI have backgrounds that can only be described as lower-income and disadvantaged if not poverty-stricken. Because they know that U.S. society is not likely to change soon, they realize that the only way for now to break out of these backgrounds is to achieve a higher income level. For most poor people, an income means a job. There are jobs, of course, which pay wages that do nothing to lift you above the poverty level; in fact, they may keep you there, and you will never even come close to the American Dream that way. There are other jobs which pay higher wages, but they require skilled people, and so education is the answer. For Indian people, who suffer the highest unemployment rate (over 60 percent) in the nation, SIPI has been an answer.

Southwestern Indian Polytechnic Institute opened its doors to Indian students in the fall semester of 1971 on 164 acres of land on the western bank of the Rio Grande in Albuquerque, New Mexico. The opening of the Institute, which had cost $13.5 million to build and equip, was lauded as a sincere and serious commitment by the BIA to make available technical-vocational education to Indian people nationwide.

Since the BIA, established in the nineteenth century, is the colonial Indian agent—so to speak—it has always had a stormy role in Indian affairs. In fact, SIPI was built originally to placate Pueblo Indian protests against BIA's closure of Santa Fe Indian School, an elementary and secondary boarding school. The federal agency had also been administering a relocation program since the early 1950s which was intended to remove Indian people from their rural homelands to U.S. urban areas. Ostensibly, Indian people would receive on-the-job training upon arrival in the city, move up the American Dream ladder, and finally flow into the mainstream.

Because Indian people soon experienced the trauma of moving from a familiar cultural context to a strange, often unfriendly one, they protested the program. They also felt that their reservation populations were being depleted at an alarming rate by the relocation of their people, and they surmised it was another attempt to take their lands once they were thinly populated. The relocation program was aimed primarily at supplying urban labor markets, which already had an excess of unskilled, unemployed people. To Indian people of the Southwest, it seemed logical that skills training could be achieved nearer to home than Dallas, Chicago, Cleveland, or Los Angeles, which was where people on "relocation" were usually sent. Although originally intended to be the Indian boarding school asked for by Pueblo Indian leaders, SIPI very quickly became the ray of hope for upgrading the postsecondary-educational and job-skills levels of Indian people. Not only would Pueblo and other southwestern Indian people have the opportunity to gain necessary training, but the school would serve national Indian educational needs as well.

The philosophy for the school derived simply from the desire of Indian people to acquire technical and vocational skills needed to become productive individuals capable of economic survival. The job market of that era was surveyed and a curriculum was designed to meet occupational demands.

SIPI, accredited by the North Central Association of Colleges and Schools since 1975, offers forty-eight certificates and degrees. A two-year degree option is also available in cooperation with the nearby University of Albuquerque. Transfer of SIPI credits is also possible to other colleges and universities. Operated on a semester basis, training programs range from six to twenty-two months.

Although employment opportunities and openings have fluctuated according to national economic conditions over the past twelve years, SIPI's student placement record indicates that its program has been highly successful. For example, even in the midst of the turmoil caused by the announcement that the school was to be closed, SIPI administrators cite the following percentages of job placement upon completion of course work by students in the school year of 1981–82. Accounting and data entry show 94 percent, secretarial and clerical 89 percent, marketing 54 percent, civil engineering and drafting 68 percent, electronics 67 percent, food preparation and management 77 percent, optical technology 89 percent, and telecommunications 67 percent, for an overall average placement rate of 73 percent of all students who have completed the course work in their chosen occupational fields. This figure compares favorably with the national rate of 70–80 percent, according to Ohio State University's National Center for Research in Vocational Education. With SIPI evidently a relative success, students, faculty and staff, the Board of Regents, and proponents of Indian education in general could not comprehend why James Watt, the Secretary of the Interior, overseer of the BIA, would move to shut down the school.

Immediately upon assuming the U.S. presidency in January 1981, Ronald Reagan implemented his budget policy of cutbacks and in many cases total elimination of funding for health, education, and social-welfare programs. Like all poor people, Indians were particularly victimized by the trimming of the national budget. A 10-percent decrease in the overall BIA budget was announced, translating into an $880-million cut which would begin in the federal fiscal year 1982.

One of the initial budget items recommended for elimination was funding for SIPI. Ken Smith, who is Indian (though others would prefer to disclaim him) and Interior's Assistant Secretary for Indian Affairs, made the recommendation in a June 15, 1981, memo to Secretary Watt. The SIPI Board of Regents passed a resolution in mid-August strongly opposing the shutdown of the school. The members began to alert Indian tribal leaders and the New Mexico congressional delegation, expressing their opposition to the planned closing of the only Indian technical-vocational school in the nation. The New Mexico Commission on Indian Affairs voted to support SIPI's efforts to stay open. Dr. John Olguin, Director of the Commission, commented that "the BIA is making a unilateral decision. It always seems the minorities and the poor suffer with these cuts." Indian people were never consulted by the BIA, although federal law requires consultation in matters dealing with Indian education.

At that point in the summer of 1981, the funding cut was a recommendation, as was pointed out by Carl Shaw, a spokesman for Assistant Secretary Smith. He claimed he understood SIPI was built to accommodate 650 students but that in 1980 there had been 250 enrolled, adding that it would be sensible to close the school for budget purposes. Acting SIPI President Tom Patterson denied Shaw's claim, stating that the school was actually operating at capacity, as it had been for some time. Additionally, Patterson referred to a BIA auditor's report showing that SIPI placed only 10 percent of its students in jobs, noting that the report was in gross error. "Our placement rate is actually more like 80 percent," he said. By then, it was clear the BIA was gathering evidence, no matter how much in error it might be, which it would need to justify any eventual decision it would make in the future about SIPI.

By early September, enough attention had been drawn to the possible closing of SIPI that Representative Manuel Lujan (Republican–New Mexico) visited the school. Afterward he called Secretary Watt to object to the recommendation for SIPI's closure. He had also talked with Assistant Secretary Smith, who told him that the costs of education at SIPI were excessive. Lujan learned on his visit to the school that the cost per student each year averaged $5,700, including room and board. Meanwhile, Senator Harrison Schmitt (Republican–New Mexico) announced that he had been assured, presumably by Watt, that Indian people would be consulted before there was any decision made to close the Institute. Indian students were not reassured by the announcement, especially since, in September, the Department of the Interior's fiscal year 1983 budget sent to the Office of Management and Budget (OMB) did not include SIPI funding.

They held a rally in the fall at which they spoke in support of SIPI's continuance, hoping that it would not cease to operate, since it represented their chance for gainful employment. Randall Sunday, an SIPI student, told the assembly, "If we lose SIPI, it's like losing a reservation." Students began to make plans to get parents, tribal leaders, friends, and supporters to contact congressional representatives and government officials and express their opposition to closure. By the middle of fall, there had been extensive reaction generated by Smith's recommendation, so that on November 16 he had to write an appeals memo to the OMB passback of the fiscal year 1983 budget. It read, "We are reversing the decision on closing Southwestern Indian Polytechnic Institute. . . ." It was a respite from the threat of closure.

It's a good thing no one foolishly claimed victory for Indian education, because on December 30, Interior Secretary Watt informed Representative Lujan that funding for SIPI would not be included in the Administration's fiscal year 1982–83 budget. Subsequently, Lujan announced that the 1981–82 school year would be the last year the school would operate. With spring semester starting in a few days, SIPI had 550 students enrolled, the largest number in its short history.

Immediately following the dictate that Southwestern Indian Polytechnic Institute was to be closed, proponents of the school lodged protests against the Department of the Interior's decision and began to organize. Del Lavato, Chairman of the All Indian Pueblo Council (AIPC), a federation of the nineteen New Mexico pueblos, went to Washington, D.C., to meet with congressional leaders to try to persuade them to restore SIPI funding for fiscal year 1982–83. Ron Mills, a Xerox service manager, who had been working since the previous summer to organize Albuquerque business support for SIPI, said there was a united front of industry representatives and the Indian community committed to saving SIPI. Some of the industries joining the fight were Hewlett-Packard, Honeywell, IBM, Sandia National Laboratories, Safeway, Mountain Bell, Cheyenne Enterprises, and Dataco.

Hearings were held February 23 through March 4, 1982, in Washington, D.C., before the Senate and House appropriations subcommittees. Senator Schmitt testified that SIPI "provides the means by which the Indian, regardless of tribal affiliation or geographic residence, can gain highly technical skills in an environment which is sensitive to cultural background, and it provides industry with a pool of trained technicians from which they actively recruit."

The SIPI Board of Regents representative testified that it was the worst time to close SIPI, because Indian unemployment was 60 percent to 85 percent nationwide, and that the proposal for closure was being made over the protest of Indian tribes who were not ever consulted, especially considering that SIPI represented a trust and treaty obligation of the U.S. Government to provide education. In his testimony, the SIPI student senate president, Daniel Ringlero, asked, "Where will these young people go? Back to our reservations to join the growing number of unemployed?"

Notwithstanding the ongoing efforts to save SIPI, on February 22 the BIA issued a memorandum organizing the closedown of SIPI by June 15, 1982.

Suddenly SIPI lost all of its New Mexico congressional support for remaining an Indian institution. Republican Senators Domenici and Schmitt and Representatives Lujan and Skeen all agreed to support Watt's plan to turn SIPI over to the non-Indian Albuquerque Technical-Vocational Institute. Even All Indian Pueblo Council Chairman Del Lavato inexplicably agreed to it. The Navajo Nation leadership also expressed support for it initially but withdrew it shortly afterward. Watt had somehow gotten the congressional delegates and Lavato to come around to his position. He was determined to take SIPI out of Indian hands. But the Congress, inspired by Representative Sydney Yates (Democrat–Illinois), disagreed, and the school was kept open for one more year.

Elmer Atencio is a counselor at SIPI. He has been through the past two years of uncertainty, puzzlement, and constant change of affairs, all of it a mad struggle to keep SIPI alive. He has taken a leave of absence to do some graduate work. We sit in a noisy restaurant near the University of New Mexico campus. His little daughter plays as we talk.

Elmer says, "In the long run, it is cheaper to educate Indian people. Because once they become trained in a skill, they can get jobs and become wage earners and taxpayers. If a person from Window Rock went to work in Gallup, he earns an income which supports four to ten people. That's the amount that the government doesn't have to provide in support. If skills training is not provided, people are kept at the same levels, unskilled; they can't go out and get jobs. It makes more sense in the long run to provide skills to people who need them.

"No other school is willing to tackle the kind of educational problems that Indian people have. Most schools, including TVI and UNM, do not address this issue because they don't want to work with remedial education. Yet there is a whole segment of the population who needs remedial education. SIPI gets a wide spectrum of students. At TVI, some of them would be lost. TVI is a very good school and it addresses the job-training needs of the white, Chicano, and black population, but it doesn't address the specific needs of the Indian population. We have tried and succeeded. We have a higher job-placement rate than TVI.

"I think Watt and the BIA believe that SIPI's educational

programs are not successful. They look at numbers. They don't
look at the people themselves. BIA was told to cut back 10
percent on all programs, and so since SIPI supposedly had a
poor record, it was earmarked for cutoff. That's the whole
trend. We're led to believe we are on the road to self-determina-
tion. When you take everything a person has and say, 'Now you
can self-determine,' the person is in worse shape than before.
One of the things that the Reagan administration keeps saying
is, 'We're doing something for the economy,' which in fact it's
not. An improved economy would have people working, and
you're not going to have people working if they're not trained.
You don't need people dependent on social-welfare programs,
which is what results when there's no work. Now is the time to
help Indians become self-sufficient by providing education programs.

"There is a force which has been important in inspiring Indian people in this struggle, and that is spiritual force. That
probably had more to do with the resistance put up than anything else. There were marches in South Dakota and here.
Medicine men performed prayers for all Indian people. Con-
gressman Yates was affected by that spirituality in my opinion,
and he has been fighting Watt all this time on behalf of SIPI.
When Watt pushes for something, he'll fight it to the ground; he
has to win the battle, no matter what it's for. If you take a look at
the SIPI issue, it's not really a big issue at all. There are bigger
issues at stake with the environmentalists and the Bureau of
Indian Affairs as a whole. But the SIPI issue has become an
obsession with Watt."

I'm reminded of the nineteenth century and the misguided
philosophy of Manifest Destiny. The role of the civilized, Western, white man was to civilize the Indian and the wild land.
Though the belief seemed to have some good intentions, it was
pitifully ignorant. Except for a perceptive few, it never occurred to its proponents that it was all part of an exploitative,
imperialistic venture. "Civilizing" was done with religious zeal
for materialistic gain. Often, the men and women who had the
most contact with Indians were Christian missionaries; even
military men who fought Indians and imprisoned them on res-

ervations held the rigid conviction that their duty was God-ordained. The ideas and actions of Secretary Watt and the Reagan administration remind me of that unholy era in U.S. history.

It is now 1983, and the problem of closure facing SIPI is no nearer a resolution than it was a year ago. Funding was received for SIPI's 1983–84 operation, but Indian students have been told by President Reagan's spokespersons this is absolutely the last year it will exist.

A younger friend recently called me up to invite me to be a part of a gathering of organizers, students, political activists, and cultural workers. I'm not sure where I fit now, but I know I've fit into any of those designations at some point in my life. I'm sure that as a writer, I easily enough am able to place myself in any of those identities. More important than the assumption of an identity, though, is what my responsibilities are as a writer, a citizen of this nation, and an Indian.

As a writer, I've written poetry, prose fiction, and essays on history, culture, literature, and language, and I've written children's stories. Usually, I've written about Indian people and their lives, because that is what I know. I've tried to regard the revelations I've made as a window into the life of all humanity, all life, primarily my motive being to reveal all people to each other so that the human community may be reaffirmed as one that is loving, compassionate, and respectful, and wise. Maybe I'm a fool for being so idealistic, but strangely I don't feel foolish.

As a citizen of this nation, I firmly believe in changing it. My belief and faith is that if you truly love this land and people, you will struggle to change it. And it must be changed; it has gone on too long toward self-destruction.

Indian people truly love this earth. You can tell it in their eyes, their voices, their hand motions. It is something, that love, that you can't describe. It is like breathing air, drinking water, being able to walk on the ground; you can't do anything, say anything, think or feel anything unless you acknowledge that

it is the earth-life-force all around you that makes it possible.
This is where the crux is: we must save the white man in order to
save ourselves. He must be taught to regard life as precious and
sacred. Maybe Indian people are fools, but we don't think so.

Christmas Eve

DAVID BRADLEY

THE BELLS WAKE ME.

My neighborhood, while unquestionably united on the subject of religion, is ineluctably divided on points of ethnicity; there is a passionate rivalry between the several Catholic churches in the area. The conflict is, at least ostensibly, friendly, and is usually private: the only time Jews, Protestants, and other heretics get caught in the cross fire is in the early morning—just about dawn in the winter—when the chimes of the various steeples let fly at thirty paces in what seems to be a carillon arrangement of "The Dueling Banjos," played, unfortunately, in totally unrelated keys. The duel usually ends in a cacophonous draw.

After six months in the neighborhood I grew used to the daily round of holy strife, and reached the point where I could snore accompaniment without even having the sacred gonging inject itself into my last desperate prewaking dreams. But this morning the bells wake me. For a moment I lie there trying to figure out what has happened. Then I realize that one set of chimes has gone on after the others have ceased, rendering a mechanical and hesitating chorus of "Hark! the Herald Angels Sing." It's not that bad, really, if you like bells. Certainly it is a marked improvement over the earlier confusion. But I am not properly appreciative. I just lie there wondering if this new reverberation can be ascribed to religious fervor that is both appropriate and commendable, given the season, or if one congregation has scraped up enough cash to buy some new bells, an escalation of arms that will have to be matched by the other congregations, perhaps by a beefing up of troop strength and volume of the drum-and-bugle corps in the Pulaski Day parade or, worse, a purchase of carillons of equal throw weight, which will wake me up in the morning until my body can adjust to the increased level of tension.

To make that scenario even less attractive is the fact that the clocks of the Archdiocese are running fast; it is not until after the last bell has bonged that my clock radio, itself set a bit ahead, clicks on, playing the closing strains of the "Hallelujah Chorus." I lie there listening to the Mormon Tabernacle Choir being joyful (a minor miracle, given the geography of Utah) to the accompaniment of the Philadelphia Orchestra, without feeling the least bit like singing along, or even getting out of bed. Handel's final crescendo is followed by the cultured-pearl voice of an announcer informing me that I am tuned to the classical music stations of the Delaware Valley, that it is Friday, December 24, 1982, and that, at the sound of the tone, the time will be 7 A.M.

At the sound of the tone, I get out of bed.

On my way to the kitchen, I switch on my stereo system, which is set up for FM and tuned to the same station as my clock radio. They are into the snobby commercials for ten-carat South African diamonds and Aryan-ideal automobiles that seem to be the advertising staple of classical-music stations these days. I often wonder what genius of marketing demographics proved that people who enjoy Beethoven and Bartók are turned on by De Beers and Mercedes-Benz. It's getting so that every time I play a symphony I feel like a decadent exploiter of the proletariat. Especially when I play it on my stereo system.

My stereo system is not the most elaborate or expensive, but it is also not minimal or cheap. When I was younger I sang in choirs and choruses, played in bands. I don't have time now, but I love music too much to enjoy bad sound. And so my system has a receiver powerful enough to strike terror into the heart of any downstairs neighbor, a turntable with a strobe light that looks sexy as hell in the dark, a cassette deck with more meters, indicators, and controls than a medium-sized executive jet, and four sets of speakers, each one of which is approximately the size of a full-grown Doberman. It cost me, depending on how you do the accounting, a month's pay, two months' take-home pay, or a year and a half of scrounging. Plus five minutes of guilt, which I experienced while transporting the cold cash from the bank (where they didn't believe I could have that much on deposit) to the store (where they were eager to give me a discount for cash and so avoid paying tribute to Mastercard) through the beggars, blind men, bag ladies, and unclassified specimens of broke and broken-down citizenry that seemed to pop up out of the pavement like targets on an advanced-level pistol range, each one with a look in his or her eye that said they knew about the wad of hundreds in my pocket, which I was about to squander on conspicuous gadgetry. When I left the stereo store I went with the delivery truck, out the back way.

Not that I let it bother me that there were people on the streets of Philadelphia who were short of such luxury items as shoes and protein and medical care while I was blowing cash on the essentials, like dual motor drive and Dolby noise reduction —at least, not for very long. I normally don't even think about the fact. But, for some ridiculous reason, the media, even classical music stations that earn their shekels flogging Caribbean cruises and Perrier water, find that Advent makes stories about the poor and down-trodden irresistible. And so, after the last attempt to make me run right out and buy a diamond from South Africa to show her I'd marry her all over again, I get treated to a Christmas Eve edition of the local news, a series of soft-hearted shinola about how the hundred and eighty thousand or so Philadelphians who are out of work are still doing their best to support the economy by buying what they can for Christmas, and how the eighty thousand or so who are afraid that they are going to lose their homes when the banks foreclose (which they won't do, since nobody could afford to buy what they foreclosed on) are nevertheless singing "Good King Wenceslas" and visiting the old folks at homes. The voice of the announcer is sugarplums, in an attempt, I suppose, to make the listener feel all warmhearted and gooey. It makes me think of doing something symbolic, like buying stock in General Public Utilities, and makes me crave my morning coffee. I turn another switch, throwing the sound into the speakers in the kitchen, and go in after it like the Marines hitting the beach at Guadalcanal.

Back in '77 a woman changed my life; she gave me a Krupp electric coffee grinder. At the time, I thought it was a stupidly bourgeois gift, a reflection of how her values had been warped by a decade of marriage to a successful doctor. (She *drove* a Mercedes-Benz, and yet thought that classical music was the overture to *William Tell*, which she called "The Lone Ranger." So much for marketing studies.) In fact, I did not appreciate the gift at all. I was poor then. Not poverty-stricken—I had a job that gave me a sufficient income to pay my bills, and I had a place to live and enough to eat, but there was not a lot left over for luxury items; I had to save up to buy a bottle of bourbon. What I didn't appreciate about the gift was that it forced me to spend money I didn't really have on otherwise unnecessary apparatus. If you have a coffee grinder, you have to have a coffee maker, and of course, you have to have coffee beans. In order to find those, I had to venture into places that I was not accustomed to even thinking about; I was living in Manhattan's East Village at the time, and in order to find unground beans I ended up going all the way over to the West Village, to Balducci's, which was and is the kind of boutique grocery store where they take American Express cards.

What I discovered in Balducci's was not that there were an awful lot of affluent folk who are both long enough on cash and short enough on brains to spend five bucks on a four-ounce can of what could, in all honesty, be called sardines—I *knew* that— but that there were all kinds of different coffees, from all kinds of places, and that they cannot be described properly by commercial brand names, whether Maxwell House or Hills Brothers, and that they all taste different, and most taste good, and none of them tastes worse than the very best instant.

This was, in a sense, heresy.

I was, at the time, an instant-coffee drinker. It was a point not only of practice but of ideology; I thought I liked the taste of instant coffee. I thought the world would be a better place if people stopped wasting time with the bourgeois ostentations of filter paper and got down to the honest peasant essentials: a jar and a spoon and a cup of hot water.

But when I started making my own coffee from scratch, or rather, from bean, I found that the taste was better. Worse, from an ideological point of view, that there was more to it than taste, or, rather, something that involved taste in a larger sense. Mak-

ing coffee put a touch of elegance into my mornings. That touch
of elegance made up for a whole lot of the austerity in the rest of
the day. Over the years, I have gone from elegance to fetishism:
I make my morning coffee with the best materials and with the
most precise measurements, so that, no matter how much of
what goes on during the rest of the day is out of my control and
even of my understanding, I can look back to my morning
coffee and know that there was something at the beginning that
was as precise and as solid and as right as I could make it.

And so, on this Christmas Eve, I use the Krupp to grind beans
grown in a mountain monastery in West Africa and measure
them into the filter cone of my Chemex, wet them down, pause,
and then pour in spring water heated in a copper pot, while my
stereo system provides the background. Which, unfortunately,
is not music, but the national news.

The national news is an example of why I care so much about
my coffee. It is out of my control, out of my understanding, and
about as far from precise, solid, and perfect as you can get. It is
vaguely amusing. And it is as ancient as the season.

There is talk of new taxes. The decree may not be going out
from Caesar Augustus, but all the world is surely taxed, and a lot
of poor Joes are putting up in stables with their pregnant wives
after hauling ass to the tax collector. No mention is made of the
market in frankincense or myrrh, but gold prices are up, which
is bad news for the Wise Men. Worse, it seems that following
stars is not as lucrative as it once was: the earthbound explorers
at the Jet Propulsion Laboratory have announced that the wan-
ing of interest in planetary exploration has forced them into
doing work for the Defense Department. The lame-duck session (aren't they all?) of whichever Congress it is (does it matter?) has accomplished exactly what you would expect from a
quacking cripple—although in the spirit of the season they have
passed another continuing resolution, so that, like the rest of
America, they can deal with the bills of Yuletide spending next
January. But their Christmas spirit is outdone by that of that
Jolly Fellow in the White House, who, taking his cue from both
religious and secular myths, has decided to rename the most
powerful engine of destruction ever designed by man the
Peacekeeper, has wrapped up economic depression in a nice

bow and called it a period of consolidation, and has decided to give the Pentagon everything on its umptibillion-dollar Christmas list. The only thing that seems to have him stymied is how to punish the poor. The traditional coal in the stocking probably seems too much like the government giving the lazy buggers something for nothing.

I am, I realize as I watch the water drip through the Chemex, in a mood as bitter as boiled coffee. The cause of it is not my premature awakening, courtesy of the Archdiocese, or the most recent accounts of the actions of a chief executive who thinks human existence is a B movie. The cause is the season. On this morning a process that began long before has reached culmination; I hate Christmas.

I have not really liked Christmas since, at the age of five or six, I tumbled onto the fact that there was no magical Santa Claus turning out endless goodies somewhere near the Pole, and further, that the source of Christmas largesse was mainly the same father who, come January, was going to be sweating bullets over how to pay the light bill. Knowing that took the fun out of things.

Later, when I became an adult, I found that the thrill of giving somebody the precisely *right* gift could easily be outweighed by the agony of giving anybody something they did not want, or need, or even like, and my feelings toward Christmas turned into true hatred. That bore fruit one December night about five years back when, fortified with a couple of shots of bourbon and confronted with the annual chore of making a list and checking it—and my bank balance—twice, I realized that the pattern of American Christmas is worse than absurd; it is a bizarre paradigm of American politics. At Christmas we tender money to an infrastructure of shopkeepers and manufacturers in exchange for goods which we estimate others might want or need, and which we therefore give to them, receiving in return goods which these others have secured from the same infrastructure on the basis of similar estimates, which, in all cases, ours and theirs, turn out to be accurate about 43 percent of the time. This occasions anxiety (how can we believe we're giving what is wanted when we know we're not getting what we want?) and a net loss of enjoyment both of the charitable

season and of our own funds of approximately 47.3 per cent—
which goes to the infrastructure. (The Lord loveth a cheerful
giver—but not as much as R. H. Macy.) It occurred to me that
night that we would all come out ahead if we gave checks (the
banks would take a cut, but a lot less than Macy's). Or better yet,
just buy ourselves what the hell we wanted.

That was partly sham. The truth was, five years back, I hated
Christmas because I could not afford to give people what I
wanted to give them. It was the one time of the year I wished to
be a millionaire. And now I should more or less love it for the
same reason. Not that I'm exactly in the chips, but times have
been good to me in the last year or so. High interest rates are
dandy when you've kept your money in the bank instead of on
your back, and when your job is at least as secure as the San
Andreas Fault. This Christmas I have bought nice things for
those I really am close to. I am feeling that I have not gotten
enough for my mother, but I always feel that way, and always
end up searching for one last gift. In fact I have left nobody out,
and I should be aglow with the sense of giving.

But, this morning, as I sip the coffee that does not greatly
warm or renew me, and listen as the radio, having done with
the desperate importunings of tradesmen, gets back to music—
Elizabethan carols played on period instruments that sound
suspiciously like electric guitars—I have the feeling that something is wrong.

I finish my coffee. I go and shower and dress. I turn off my
stereo and pick up my suitcase and my briefcase. I am, like any
good compulsive, on my way to the office to clean up a few
chores before I go home to my mother's for the holidays.

II

I am a teacher in the English Department of a large urban
university. I do not teach English, however. I teach writing.
When I am doing what I like to do, that means I am teaching
people how to organize their imaginings into short fiction.
When I am doing what I don't particularly like to do, I am
teaching people how to organize their thoughts and ideas into
essays. I don't particularly like to do that, not because I do not

like nonfiction but, rather, because I have noticed, over the half-dozen years I have been doing it, that the students have had less and less interest in mastering the techniques in which I can instruct them. I do not know all of the reasons for that. I only know that teaching a class in basic writing, which used to be a fairly challenging and rewarding endeavor, has become an exercise in boredom and frustration.

I do not think about that very often. When I am not at the university, I do not think about the place or what goes on—or does not go on—there. When I am there, I am busy doing things; I have no time to think. But, once or twice a semester, I end up going into my office at an odd time—late at night, on a Sunday, or after the last final exam has been given—a time when the students and most of the faculty are absent, when the university is nothing more than a collection of buildings of miscellaneous vintage on North Broad Street, cheek to jowl with a couple of classic-pattern ghettos complete with ill-conceived public housing, abandoned row houses, small businesses huddled together like circled Conestogas waiting for the Apaches to attack, and people who manage to survive, at least until they die of diseases born of violence born of despair or poverty born of indifference. I go in at those times to finish up paperwork that has been shunted aside during the more insistent day-to-day business of the semester. Usually when I start getting caught up on the paperwork I start to think, not only because the paperwork is boring but because it reminds me of all the things that I would like to forget.

This day, for example, the detritus floating on the top of my IN box is a report from the local chapter of the American Association of University Professors discussing the matter of retrenchment, the process by which professors who have been tenured can now be informed that they have eighteen months to pack up ten or fifteen years of commitment and take it on the road. At my university such warnings have gone out ostensibly because of a lack of funds. When there turned out to be no such shortfall, the administration decided that the rationale for retrenchment was that students did not seem to want to take courses in geography, ethnic studies, foreign languages, and education. The substance of the report I am reading is that nothing has changed, and, come June, the ranks of the tenured will be summarily diminished.

None of which affects me directly. There are literally scores of people in my department who are below me in rank, and they would have to be eliminated before the purge would get to me. Still, I am bothered by the report. Many of those who would go in such a purge are my friends (I have not been tenured long enough to start thinking of myself as "senior faculty") and almost all of them are more accomplished than most of the now-senior faculty were at the same age. It would grieve me greatly to know that the best and the brightest were going down the tubes in my department, as it does grieve me to know that it is happening in others. Moreover, I know that the only reason retrenchment is not happening in my department is that students are required to take composition and most of them are so poorly prepared by the secondary school system that they need at least a full semester of remedial instruction to qualify to take the comp course, let alone pass it. And the only reason other departments are facing retrenchment is that what they teach has, at my university as at so many others, ceased to be required. Now it is possible for students to graduate with honors from an appalling number of major universities without having acquired most of the skills that were once thought to be the au fait for the educated person. It is possible to get a degree without taking a single course in philosophy, history, or religion, without reading a book written before you were born, without being able to read a menu or a map or even ask the way to the bathroom in a language not your own. But what really bothers me is that the letter in my IN box requires me to do nothing but read it. Communications on the subject of retrenchment are not subject to a lot of feedback these days. Retrenchment is not a matter for discussion; it is a way of life.

The next item in my IN box is an announcement that is being sent to prospective students telling them of tuition increases, the increased difficulty in securing financial aid, the new and more stringent requirements for work-study employment, and the federal government's increasing determination to track down graduates who become delinquent in paying back their educational loans. All of which gives graphic demonstration of the reasons why students can't be forced to take philosophy any more; they can't be bothered with such frills when, nine months after graduation, some bureaucrat is going to be sending people after them to break their legs if they don't start paying off their loans.

The next item is a form letter from Edward G. Gibson, a former Skylab astronaut who is apparently heading up something called the American Space Foundation. Gibson wants me to send money to support lobbying efforts to support the space program. "I remember the immense pride and overwhelming sense of accomplishment I felt as I orbited the earth in Skylab III over 1200 times," he writes. "America's future seemed so bright, so clear." Gibson goes on to tell me that, if I send somewhere between fifteen bucks and five hundred I can stand up to the special interests and bureaucrats that are killing the space program. I wonder if he sent a letter to the Pentagon.

There is another form letter, signed by Vice-President Bush, asking for a contribution to the Republican National Committee. I wonder why the committee can't solve its financial problems using the same kinds of policies Bush once called "voodoo economics."

I move on through the mail, the circulars from publishers advertising fifteen books on writing that will arrest the decline in our national ability to express our needs and desires, the announcements of organizing meetings for literally dozens of committees to "discuss ways to meet the threat posed by the Administration's attitudes toward" integration or justice or the environment or the arts or health-care services or fiscal responsibility or world peace or alternative energy sources or affirmative action or women's rights or birth-control information or abortion or funds for education and job training or day care or welfare or whatever.

There is a letter from a student, asking for advice on what to do about registering for the draft. He has heard that, if he does not register, the government will be cutting off his scholarship. And there is another letter, dated October, that I must have somehow missed when it first came in. It is from a former student named Nancy.

Nancy was a very special student. She was an older woman, in her mid-thirties when she was a junior, five or six years ago. She had gotten pregnant in her teens because nobody had taught her about birth control, and she had had the child because in those days abortion was illegal. She had kept it because she had found out that a black child's chances for a swift and successful adoption were less than the best, and she had raised the child alone because she decided that the father was not the man she would like to spend her life with or have her child influenced by. She had lived on welfare and had finished high school through correspondence courses. When the child was old enough for school, Nancy had gotten a job as a secretary. Eventually she had decided that she was not going to get anywhere and had started going to night school, working full time and raising the child at the same time. When I met her she had decided to take a chance, had quit her job, put together a kind of financial aid package of her savings, loans, and money from Aid to Families with Dependent Children, and enrolled full time, making a final charge for her degree. She had graduated with honors and had moved to Ohio, where she had been offered a teaching job.

When last I heard from Nancy everything had been going right. Her daughter was in high school, looking toward college. Nancy had married, and she and her husband had purchased a house. She was enjoying teaching and was working on her Ph.D.

Nancy's is a newsy letter. She congratulates me on a book I've published, says she hopes I'm making lots of money. She's doing well, she says. Her husband was laid off six months ago and for a while it looked as if they were going to lose the house, but she found a second job as a waitress. Her daughter was upset because she couldn't help out in the crisis, but Nancy knows she tried. It's enough that her daughter has been so cheerful about putting off college for a couple years. Nancy, of course, had to give up graduate school, but she will go back as soon as things get better, although, to be honest, she's not sure she sees the point. I put her letter down. I stand up from my desk and stretch, looking out my window. I do not know what to write to Nancy.

I could tell her that I have done very well this year. I have won literary prizes. I have published my work in good places. I have made a little money. I have gotten tenure, and a promotion, and a small raise. Nancy would be happy for me. But I can't tell her any of it, because in the context of her letter, of her life, my success seems disgustingly relative. You might even say I'm getting ahead.

But I do not want to get ahead. I want to prosper. I am no fool. But I do not want to feel, as I do now feel, that there is something suspect about my every comfort. I do not mind being head above the crowd, but I do mind standing on its shoulders.

My office is on the eleventh floor, and my window affords me a view of the city that is stunning at night, when the lights provide the dots for the imagination to draw lines to connect and the darkness hides the real shape of what lies below. But now it is not dark. It is not night. It is the bright afternoon of the Eve of Christmas, slouching toward a winter dusk.

III

Riding west with Amtrak, across the belly of the state, along the route of the once-mighty Pennsylvania Railroad, since merged, bankrupted, denatured, and combined with other feebled roads, its logotype a legend fading on leased-out cars, its name a memory. The road was born in the 1840's; ten years back it died. But the tracks remain.

At the limits of Philadelphia the tracks form the spine of the old Main Line, a string of towns noted for Anglo-Saxon asceticism, Protestant pride, Republican respectability: for horse shows, dog shows, debutantes and bankers, lawyers and martinis and a patrician sort of public-spiritedness. No matter who's in power, these are the folks, along with their old prep school chums from Boston and New York, who run the country, or think they do, sure that that was how God intended it to be. There are a couple of these Main Line Private Citizens across the aisle from me, lean men of substantial but not advanced age, with leather briefcases that show use but not wear. Their pinstriped suits are blue and brown, respectively. Their hair is thinning and growing lighter (balding and graying are processes too vulgar for the Main Line). Their lips are as thin as the gold watches on their wrists. They talk to each other in quiet

tones. They do not whisper; in some posh prep school they
learned the art of Anglo-Saxon Protestant communication, the
ability to listen so well and speak so quietly that the conversation is almost in code, intelligible only to others schooled in the
same technique. Compared to these men, E. F. Hutton is a
vulgar shill, wanting the world to stop and listen. These men
speak not to be overheard. Still, if you listen closely you can hear
a word or two and know that they, like Hutton, talk of stocks
and bonds and brokers. And if you listen for the sound of the
words, you can tell that they are angry and afraid.

They get off at Paoli. The train rumbles on, full of poorer folk,
the tracks taking it out toward Lancaster, the Amish time-warp
zone of bonnets, one-horse shays. (There are Amishmen on the
train, seeming as worried in their black suits as the Main Liners
in their pin-striped blue and brown.) After Lancaster the tracks
follow the Susquehanna, past the eerie hyperbolic towers of
Three Mile Island (where, so General Public Utilities and the
NRC say, everything is under control now; just like it was before) through Middletown, where there is not a trace of radia-
tion or the aftereffects of near-destruction, except that the people seem to have either total, unflagging, unremitting faith in
their leaders, or absolutely none at all.

Then comes Harrisburg, the state capital, where folks had a
scare of their own a few months back, when an able incumbent
Republican governor, so popular he smiled even off camera, so
secure that CBS News featured him as a politician in no trouble,
so confident that aides dared to speak of the vice-presidency,
found himself, as the election night tallies came in, hanging by
his fingernails at the edge of a sudden abyss, as voters used him
unmercifully as Ronald Reagan's whipping boy.

And then the tracks will reach into the mountains, toward
towns of coal and steel. At the far side, Pittsburgh, where Carnegie made his millions and gave them away, while the workers
fought with his Pinkertons over who should have the profits
distilled from their sweat. Now they get twenty-five bucks an
hour. Or would, but there are hardly any profits, and precious
little sweat; the jobless lines are long in Pittsburgh, and the hit
tune is a tuneless variation on a theme of foreign steel, and men
who went on strike with arrogance are praying for their pride.

They are praying too in Johnstown, a hundred miles nearer the center of the state. They are going to lose nearly three thousand jobs in Johnstown, a town of about fifty-five thousand. They thought they were safe—their steel plant was modern, electrified—but Bethlehem Steel is packing the whole thing up and moving it. The people will not move; nobody in Pennsylvania moves; they are the least mobile people of any state in the union. What they will do is hard to say.

I will not have to look at Johnstown; my stop is Altoona, thirty-nine miles closer, an hour and five minutes sooner, and a decade, maybe two, more precocious. Altoona was a railroad town, laid out by the Pennsy as a switching point back in 1849. For a hundred years and more it prospered as a crossroads. The governors met there to pledge support for President Lincoln; Charles Dickens wrote about it in *American Notes;* all the vaudevillians made bad jokes about it, even as they played its halls. But it was always a creature of the railroad. Rolling stock was built in Altoona, in the largest car shops in the world, and the freights that came from Pittsburgh laden with bituminous and Bessemer paused for fuel and water and to have their journal boxes repacked with oily waste. The passenger trains stopped too, and waited while the helper engines coupled on to push the Pullmans up the mountains and around the Horseshoe Curve.

Twenty-five years ago I grew sleepless at the thought of Altoona, where from my home, a tiny town forty miles away, I would go at odd hours when my mother took my father to or from the train. We would sit outside the station, a failing but determined building, its red bricks purpled by a century of smoke, and watch the men in pin-striped caps as they walked along the trains with long-handled hammers, lifting the lids of journal boxes, checking for bearings run hot and dry, and then coming back into a tiny little house at the edge of the tracks. Through the window you could see them pouring coffee from an enormous metal pot.

The trains were lovely. They had names that spanned history and geography and culture: the Liberty, the National, and the Leni-Lenape Limiteds, the Congressional, the Senator, the Broadway Limited, the Spirit of St. Louis. The engines were great, black, bellowing things that tamed suddenly as they coasted into the station. The baggage cars behind them were dull green or brown or gray, but then would come the purple day coaches, silver sleepers, diners, and round-ended observation cars with their red marker and white running lights, all of them lit up like Christmas. As they slowed, you could look through the windows at the men who worked them, standing in the mail car sorting letters through the night, or leaning in the open doors of gleaming kitchens, nonchalant and unafraid.

Twice my father took me with him West, all the way to Chicago, making sure that we had a roomette in the rear of the train and on the side from which I could look out the window and see the locomotive as it pulled us around the Horseshoe Curve. And a half a dozen times he took me to the East, rolling down from the mountaintops on the smooth and shining rails.

The rails are rusty now, and hardly smooth. The ballast has settled, the ties have rotted, and the spikes that hold the rails down suffer from metal fatigue, and between Lancaster and Harrisburg the train shakes like a dipso with DT's. They call it the Broadway Limited, but it's not. The elegance is gone, and the engine is apologetic. There is no observation car—the last car is just a day coach with its rear door sealed and locked, like the cauterized stump of an amputated limb. Still, this is a better train than most. There is a diner and a sleeper and a baggage car. It's the only train from Philly to Pittsburgh that offers those ancient amenities. (There's only one other train, anyway.) And it's the only one that reaches out to Chicago.

As I ride it westward, thinking of the tales my father would tell me of the trains that bellowed smoke and cinders, and of the sudden cleanliness and quiet when the diesels came, it occurs to me that we are going backward. That, once, these tracks were the pathways of our progress, and now they are the harbingers of stagnation. I wonder what we've come to, that the steel that linked our cities has turned to rust from sheer disuse.

It is a stupid thought, of course. When my father and I rode the trains together, the commercial jet was a gleam in an engineer's eye, and Dwight Eisenhower was still trying to sell Congress on the concept of the Interstate. There are only two trains between Philly and Pittsburgh, because you can drive yourself there in the same time even if you don't speed, and TWA can get you there inside an hour. So can U.S. Air. The tracks replaced canals, and that was progress. They have been replaced by lines of concrete and the open sky. There is nothing to lament.

Yet I know the concrete is cracked and broken in a million places, that the bridges are not what they were, and that the high-speed promise of the Interstate has become a fading dream. If I had a son, we would drive the Turnpike at a sedate fifty-five, and I would tell him tales of the good old days, when we cruised at seventy. And I know too that the promise of the skies is not what it once was, and that if I had a son I would tell him how when I was his age I dreamed of flying to another world, and how, by God, we did it, in the summer of '69. True, it was only the moon, a puddle jump in celestial terms, but it was a step toward the stars, and at the age of nineteen I cried because of the beauty of it. By then I knew I would never go myself, but in a sense I did go; we all did. We went back to the moon before the year was out, sent our robots scampering like bird dogs toward the sands of Mars, and a scientist detected the waves of gravity, and maybe we would make the stars after all.

We did not. We turned back, or aside, or something. We have not abandoned space, but we build shuttles to service satellites —ships not for great leaps into the darkness, but for the chore of mending wall. Our astronauts have become delivery-truck drivers, transporting packages for hire. The new Age of Exploration is the Age of Federal Express. And the earthbound dreamers who built the probes that at least sent our eyes to Mars and Jupiter and Saturn are going to build seeing-eye dogs for bombs.

And so, I think I would tell my son, if I had one, those were the good old days. Which was just what my father told me. And he was wrong. In his good old days *his* father died of diabetes a year before they discovered insulin. In his good old days people died of cancer automatically, and children limped from polio, and people coughed their lungs out from TB. But the TB rate is up again. And we can't get a handle on lung cancer, not because the doctors can't deal with it but because some selfish bastards refuse to let happen to tobacco what happened to cyclamates, while they patter piously about American values and prayer in the schools. And so, son, when I tell you that the good old days are gone, perhaps I'm right. After all, the best minds of my generation are designing video games.

IV

At the very brink of Christmas I find another gift for my mother that really makes her happy: I decide to go with her to church.

For years it was a kind of a tradition that I would accompany my mother to the midnight candlelight and carol service at the local Methodist church. But then modernism infected the Methodists; the ancient and familiar scriptures had been scrapped in favor of some sentimental slop that sounded as if it had been dashed off in a Hollywood hot tub, and the traditional hymns, with their words by the Apostles and music by the greatest composers of all time, had been virtually eliminated in order to make room for "contemporary carols," with lyrics by Hallmark and *Reader's Digest,* and tunes by Barry Manilow. And the climax of the service, the playing of the "Hallelujah Chorus" while the congregation left the church, carrying candles into the night, had been abandoned. It was too dangerous, they said. I realized then that I was truly a reactionary; the local congregation, despite a general conservatism, had not seemed to mind the innovations, while I declared that there was no reason for me to go to the service. My mother knows when I mean what I say, and since has gone to an earlier service so she would not have to come home late and alone.

But, this Christmas Eve, as she prepared to go, I said I would go with her if she wanted to go to the midnight service. Later, as we leave the house, I see the happiness in my mother's eyes and realize it was easy to give my mother something she wanted. What is really ironic was that I wasn't trying to do that at all. I was trying to give me something that I needed.

I do not know precisely what that something is. I only know that I am hungry for *something.* Perhaps a sense of calm and order, of precise timing, controlled reaction, of prophesies fulfilled. Or perhaps only the sense that somewhere, never mind exactly where, something good and right and fair is happening that sometime, never mind exactly when, will make itself apparent; that in some distant constellation a star has flamed to unaccustomed brilliance, and all that we must do is wait for the arrival of the light. I do not know that I am going to find anything like that in the United Methodist Church, but it is the only place that I can think of.

The town is oddly busy, oddly quiet. The square, at ten-thirty on a winter night, would usually be as empty as Siberia; tonight it is full of cars and people on their way to services at the several churches—Lutheran, Presbyterian, Episcopalian, as well as Methodist. But they make no noise. It seems as if the air were deadened by fog, the ground obscured by muffling snow. But there is no snow; it is a midnight clear. The stars shine balefully.

We are early for the service, among the first to take our bulletins and candles from the ushers and make our way down the carpeted aisle. We have our choice of pews, and lots of time to look over the order of service.

The Methodists, it would appear, have waxed weary of liturgical innovation; the service outlined is so traditional it draws not only on the Gospels, but on the Prophets. I am pleased as I busy myself with the hymnal, finding the place of the first carol. At precisely ten forty-five the organist begins the prelude.

The music, Randall Thompson's setting of "The Last Words of David," could be called modern, but I do not mind. It is one of my favorite pieces; I have sung it myself a dozen times, and hearing the notes now the words come back to me: "He that ruleth over men must be just, ruling in the fear of God." Remembering, I begin to feel a sense of happiness, and calm. But then it strikes me that this is not precisely the music one might want to begin a Christmas service, and I worry that the thing is going to be some kind of hodgepodge of dissonant elements, a service in name only.

But then I see a connection, remembering the scriptures from which those words come, passages that tell how David, as a young man appointed ruler and promised that from his loins would spring a dynasty that would endure long after he himself slept with his fathers, as an aging and willful monarch enforced a policy—the counting of his nation's fighting men—that incurred the wrath of Jehovah. Offered a multiple choice of di-

vine retribution, seven years of famine, three months of inva-
sion, or three days of pestilence, David chose pestilence. But
after seventy thousand men had died David admitted his fool-
ishness, and begged that the consequences of his actions not fall
upon the people, but against himself. He made a sacrifice, and
the plague was stayed. David, who died soon after, slept, as God
had promised he would, with his ancestors, in a place that came
to be called the City of David: Bethlehem. The connection is
there, and it reassures me; I lean back against the pew and
begin, for the first time since my morning coffee, to relax.

The church is filling quickly now. The pew just ahead of me is
occupied from one end to the other with a single family, a great-
grandmother in her eighties, a set of grandparents in their
sixties, parents in their forties, four or five children in their
teens and twenties, one daughter or daughter-in-law who is on
the way to adding still another generation. It is that kind of
congregation, that kind of town. I do not have to look around to
know that parts of that unbroken chain will be duplicated in
every pew; children come home for Christmas in this town, and
the families go to church. They have Christmas trees and deco-
rations, and they take pictures of people opening gifts. They
don't use instant cameras, because it is more important that you
get a lot of good prints from each negative than that you see
what happened right away. They are not rich people—church is
the reason many of the men own a suit, and some are on welfare
—but they are not poor, for the most part. They own their
homes and a little land, some have businesses or farms that are
run without a lot of aggressive imagination, perhaps, but with
care and responsibility, and often as family operations. They
believe in the Ten Commandments. It is still something of a
disgrace to put an aging parent in a home, and adultery, although not as uncommon as they might want you to believe, is
still a cause for scandal. They care about high school football and
wrestling and cheerleading contests and the band. The local
paper, devoting a page or two to national news, could never be
replaced by the New York *Times*. They are good people. They
are too quick to reject a new idea, too slow to accept a new-
comer to town, too fond of the way things are, too determined
to ignore any criticism of the way things used to be, but they are

steadfast in belief, accepting and understanding and willing to help their neighbors, generous with their substance, proud of their families.

I know these things about them because I am so much like them. Oh, there is a widening gulf between us. I started out as a Teen-Aged Republican, but then kept clean for Gene, rang doorbells for Hubert Humphrey, and then took passage for points to the extreme left. They were for Nixon in '60, and in '68 and '72, and Ford in '76. They really liked Goldwater and they turned handsprings for Ronald Reagan. That is just one of many ways my life has not turned out at all like theirs. In fact, it never was much like theirs, although they would not believe that, and that itself makes the gulf grow wider.

And yet in every basic way we are the same. My leftward voyage has showed me that politics, like the earth, is round; I am as conservative as they are not, perhaps more so. The only difference is, I got there not by birth or reaction, but by circumnavigation.

And so I wonder, as the prelude comes to its quiet end, and the choir comes in, if they have all come here feeling as I do, searching as I am. Is there for them a sense of being at a turning point this Christmas Eve, a sense of need? I think I can detect that in the people around me, but I am given to flights of fancy.

The service is all I had hoped that it would be. The theme of ancestry denoted by the prelude is carried through in a careful weaving of scriptures, the reading done not by the minister but by an optometrist with a clear and rhythmic voice:

"And there shall come forth a rod out of the stem of Jesse, and a Branch shall grow out of his roots: And the spirit of the Lord shall rest upon him, the spirit of wisdom and understanding, the spirit of counsel and might, the spirit of knowledge and the fear of the Lord; And shall make him of quick understanding in the fear of the Lord: and he shall not judge after the sight of his eyes, neither reprove after the hearing of his ears: But with righteousness shall he judge the poor, and reprove with equity for the meek of the earth. . . ."

Suddenly I realize what I have come here for, just exactly what is being promised. I am looking for a leader just like that. The thought frightens me. For never before in my life have I felt the need of a leader. I have always believed that I knew what needed to be done, and had a pretty good idea of how to go about it. Oh, when it came to matters of public policy I was one of the masses that the politicians always assume are treading along in the rear. But I wasn't, really. I complained. I cursed them for being fools. My idea of a good leader was someone who did what I would have done if I had had the time or the opportunity or the interest. But now, I realize, that is no longer so. It has all gotten beyond my understanding. I do not know what we should do. I do not know what I would do. And I feel fear, not only because of my helplessness, but because I know what helpless people often do: mistake the charlatan for a savior. We follow the man with the shiny boots and the simple solutions; if we do not know and know we do not know, we tend to follow those who say they know.

I see then that this is what happened to bring Ronald Reagan to power. He said he knew. He acted as though he knew, and as though all those who had come before him were fools, or thieves, or worse. He made it sound so easy to know. And now we see that he does not know. He does not even know that he does not know.

He does not really know how to fix the economy, or foreign policy. He does not know how to shrink the bureaucracy, or make government less intrusive. He does not know how to make us secure. He does not even know *us*. He underestimates our compassion. He thinks we want to end poverty only if we are poor, to provide for the aged only if we are elderly, to end inequality only if we are unequal. He thinks the employed don't worry about the unemployed, that the educated give no thought to the uneducated, that we will not mind a little mass destruction so long as we ourselves survive; he thinks we would not weep for Russia's dead. He thinks we *want* to profit from a monetary crisis, and grind the peasants beneath our carriage wheels. He thinks we are selfish and inhuman. He sells us short.

The optometrist reads the scripture, telling the old tale of shepherds who had the common sense to know a miracle when they saw it, and of wise men who had the courage to follow stars. But I think, as we sing of towns as small and quiet as the one we stand in, of choirs of angels, of peace on earth and mercy mild and thousand-year-old promises fulfilled, we are not selfish and inhuman. We are better than Ronald Reagan knows.

And we are not entirely foolish; it may take us a while to figure it out, but we know when we've been had.

And we are not really all that desperate yet. We can wait. We can find our own way yet. We do not need to cling too strongly to what we have and do not like. We don't have to stay a downward course.

I know that, because I can feel the hope and strength in the Christmas music, because I think I hear the voices around me growing stronger as we move through the old familiar carols, bringing the service to its old familiar end. The electric lights about us go out, and through the aisles come acolytes carrying tapers. They pause at the end of each pew. One person there dips his candle to theirs and then turns and sends the borrowed flame flowing down the row. It is swift as sunlight—the sanctuary is dark one moment, the next, it seems, it shouts with light. We can move that quickly when we want to, so easily defeat the dark.

And then the choir, *a capella*, begins to sing the song of joy, and we sing too. Our voices climb and heaven and nature really do seem to join in.

And when the song has ended, as if by magic the bell begins to ring. And then there is magic; the bells of the other churches ring. Somehow, in all those churches, all the different services have moved as one. I feel tears behind my eyes, in a place that no one sees, and I sense that I am not alone in that. And we stand there, silent in light of candles, listening to the bells.

When the echoes die, the minister speaks the words of prophecy that somehow make the future seem so sure:

"The people that walked in darkness have seen a great light: they that dwell in the land of the shadow of death, upon them hath the light shined. . . . For unto us a child is born, unto us a son is given: and the government shall be upon his shoulder. . . ."

And then I know that there is something wrong. For this is where, in prior years, the organ would begin the "Hallelujah Chorus," and we would take our candles out into the night. But there has been too long a hiatus; we have forgotten how it goes. When the song begins, no one moves. We stand there, each afraid to take a step. In time we become comfortable in immobility, and we stand and listen as the song plays out. When it ends, we still stand there, holding hopeful candles. Someone somewhere blows his out. Someone else does too. And then an unseen usher switches on the lights.

The basic idea for "Christmas Eve" was suggested by the assignment to "seek out those people who have been hurt by the Reagan administration, to choose a person or a family, and to write about them." A bit perversely, I suppose, I thought first of the kind of person that I wanted: an unlikely person, not the sort of welfare mother or unemployed steelworker whom you see on every other newscast; someone who was affected in an unobvious way, a way that stretched beyond a single set of policies. I wanted a person affected in a way that would be valid even if the economy straightened itself out and the Russians did invade Poland. Because to me Reaganism is bad even if it works.

The more I thought the more I realized that the person who best fulfilled my requirements was myself. I do not appear to fit the profile of one who suffers from Reagan's presidency. I am better fed, better clothed, better housed than I have ever been. I am not poor or even losing ground—I have made more money since Reagan became President than in the five years preceding the event. I am not unemployed—I have a higher degree of job security than the President himself. And I am more conservative than he is. I really believe in the principles and programs he has most abandoned: a strong, effective military; a balanced budget; involvement of the private sector; limitations on government employment, spending, and intervention.

Yet I am hurt by Ronald Reagan. Not by his principles, but by the fact that he's only mouthing the words. His is an administration without philosophical integrity, of simpleminded selfishness, rather than enlightened self-interest. It diminishes me when he invokes my values to excuse his venality. It is not surprising that that line of thought should lead me to recall John Donne's "Meditation 17," from which came the image of tolling bells that begins and ends the piece.

From that point on, "Christmas Eve" was less an exercise in political writing than a matter of artistic experimentation. Ronald Reagan was merely the excuse for it. I must say, however, that, while the piece owes a great deal to Donne and to the geography and people of Pennsylvania, the real credit goes to Ronald Reagan's stupidity. He is as good an excuse for creation as he is a poor excuse for a President. Idiots are often as inspirational as great works and great landscapes.

Such is the irony of art.

Contributors and Editors

Ronald F. Arias

Ron Arias teaches and writes. He has also worked as a journalist in Los Angeles, Caracas, and Buenos Aires. His novel *The Road to Tamazunchale* was nominated for a National Book Award. He has also published stories, reviews, and a play.

He is a member of the board of the National Endowment for the Arts Coordinating Council of Literary Magazines and a contributing editor of *The American Book Review* and the *Revista Chicano-Riquena*. After receiving his M.A. from the University of California at Los Angeles, he spent two years in the Peace Corps in Cuzco, Peru.

David Bradley

David Bradley is the author of *South Street* and *The Chaneysville Incident,* for which he received the PEN/Faulkner Award and was nominated for an American Book Award. He teaches in the English Department of Temple University.

Eric Etheridge

Eric Etheridge is from Jackson, Mississippi. He graduated from Vanderbilt University. He is currently Assistant Editor of *The Nation.*

Ernest Hebert

Ernest Hebert is a native of New Hampshire, born and raised in Keene. He graduated from Keene State College and did postgraduate work at the Stanford Writing Center. He writes a weekly column for the Boston *Globe*. His first novel, *The Dogs of March*, was cited by the Ernest Hemingway Foundation. His second novel, *A Little More than Kin*, was published in 1982.

Maxine Kumin

Maxine Kumin, a Pulitzer Prize-winning poet who was Consultant in Poetry to the Library of Congress in 1981–82, also writes essays and fiction. Her most recent collection, *Our Ground Time Here Will Be*

Brief; New & Selected Poems, was published in 1982 on the same day as her collection of short stories *Why Can't We Live Together like Civilized Human Beings?* She and her husband live on an old farm in central New Hampshire.

Simon J. Ortiz

Simon J. Ortiz is the author of four books of poetry, including *Going for the Rain* and *From Sand Creek,* three books for children, a book of essays and a book of stories, *Howbah Indians.* He has received both a Discovery Grant and a fellowship from the National Endowment for the Arts. He was a fellow in the University of Iowa International Writing Program and an Honors Fellow at the White House Salute to Poetry and American Poets in January 1980. He lives in Albuquerque, New Mexico.

David Ray

David Ray is the author of several books of poetry, including *The Touched Life.* He has also published widely in little magazines and in *The New Yorker, The Paris Review, The Atlantic Monthly, Harper's Magazine,* etc. He has been editor of *Chicago Review* and *Epoch.* He has received a Woursell fellowship, a National Endowment for the Arts fellowship for fiction, an Arvon Prize, the N. T. Veatch Award for Distinguished Research and Creativity, an Indo-U.S. fellowship, and the Thorpe Menn Award. Presently he is Professor of English and editor of *New Letters* at the University of Missouri-Kansas City.

Edward Rivera

Edward Rivera is the author of *Family Installments; Memories of Growing Up Hispanic.* He was born in Orocovia, Puerto Rico, and grew up in New York City. He attended parochial and public schools in Spanish Harlem and received his B.A. in English from City College and his M.F.A. from Columbia University. He is currently teaching English at the City College of New York.

Sylvia Sasson

Sylvia Sasson has worked in publishing in California and New York. Her reviews have been published in *Review,* the Chicago *Tribune, The Nation,* and *Publishers Weekly.* She is currently working on an oral history of the movies.

Mary Lee Settle

Mary Lee Settle's entire Beulah Quintet has recently been reissued in paperback. The novels of the quintet are *Prisons, O Beulah Land, Know Nothing, The Scapegoat,* and *The Killing Ground.* Her novel *Blood Tie* won the National Book Award in 1978. Among her other works are the novels *The Kiss of Kin, The Clam Shell,* and *The Love Eaters,* and plays, stories, articles, and an account of her years in England during World War II as a volunteer in the Women's Auxiliary of the RAF, *All the Brave Promises.* She lives in Virginia.

Earl Shorris

Earl Shorris has written three novels, *Ofay, The Boots of the Virgin,* and *Under the Fifth Sun,* and three books of nonfiction, *The Death of The Great Spirit, The Oppressed Middle—Scenes From Corporate Life,* and *Jews Without Mercy—A Lament.*

John van der Zee

John van der Zee is the author of three novels, *The Plum Explosion, Blood Brotherhood,* and *Stateline,* and three works of nonfiction, *Life in the Peace Zone, Canyon,* and *The Greatest Men's Party on Earth: Inside the Bohemian Grove.* He is at work on a book called *Bound Over,* the story of indentured servitude and its effects on American conscience. He lives with his wife and son and daughter in San Francisco.